The Insider's Guide

to

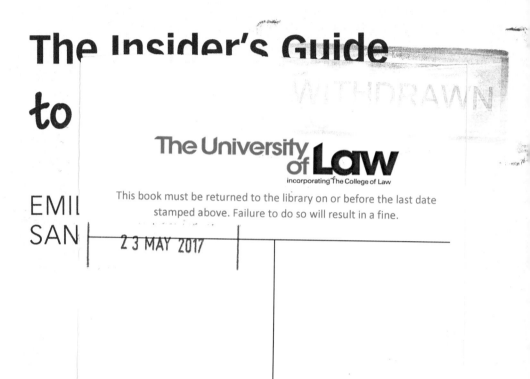

EMIL
SAN

Rou
Taylo
LONDON A

First published 2016
by Routledge
2 Park Square, Milton Park, Abingdon, Oxon, OX14 4RN

and by Routledge
711 Third Avenue, New York, NY 10017

Routledge is an imprint of the Taylor & Francis Group, an informa business

British Library Cataloguing in Publication Data
A catalogue record for this book is available from the British Library

Library of Congress Cataloging-in-Publication Data
Names: Allbon, Emily, author. | Kaur Dua, Sanmeet, author.
Title: The insider's guide to legal skills/Emily Allbon & Sanmeet Kaur Dua.
Description: New York, NY: Routledge, 2016.
Identifiers: LCCN 2015046613 | ISBN 9781138828735 (pbk) | ISBN 9781315738123 (ebk)
Subjects: LCSH: Practice of law – Great Britain – Problems, exercises, etc. | Law – Vocational guidance – Great Britain. | Legal composition.
Classification: LCC KD460.A96 2016 | DDC 347.41/0504 – dc23
LC record available at http://lccn.loc.gov/2015046613

ISBN: 978-1-138-82872-8 (hbk)
ISBN: 978-1-138-82873-5 (pbk)
ISBN: 978-1-315-73812-3 (ebk)

Typeset in Vectora LH by
Florence Production Ltd, Stoodleigh, Devon, UK

Printed and bound in Great Britain by
TJ International Ltd, Padstow, Cornwall

Contents

Authors' note

EMILY

I've been a student on four separate occasions, in very different circumstances. First as an undergraduate living on campus and then various postgraduate experiences: a full-time Master's with a weekend job, a distance learning degree while working full-time and finally another Master's part-time, combined with working full-time, but with the added challenge of being a single parent. I remember each of these experiences vividly and the difficulties that had to be overcome. These days everyone comes to education with different stories and experiences: some scarily driven, grabbing opportunities where they can, and others meandering along, content to see where life takes them.

I've been creating resources and writing for law students for well over a decade via my Lawbore website (lawbore.net), but this is my first book, and I am very excited that its focus is on legal skills. Legal skills have always been very close to my heart; as a law librarian I spent much of my time helping students with everything from finding cases and understanding legal abbreviations to gaining expertise in legal databases and referencing correctly. As an academic my role has extended of course, and alongside my teaching (Legal Method, English Legal System and Land Law) I help my students build their skills in a variety of areas.

As Moot Director I focus on building students' confidence in mooting, form teams for national and international competitions and create as many opportunities as I can for those keen to moot.

As module leader for the Legal Method module, I'm always a little disappointed that students want to gallop through this course, eager to get onto sexier core subjects like Criminal Law. The content covered by any module in Legal Method or Legal Skills is designed to set the foundations for the rest of your law degree – meaning that you can concentrate in your other subjects on learning the substantive law, not struggling with how to read a case, or find whether a particular section of an Act has been amended. Learning how to moot helps hugely with all of your subjects because you have to learn how to research, how to build an argument, write succinctly and persuasively, and present confidently. I hope this book will give you a new-found respect for legal skills and help you get a handle on these absolutely fundamental aspects of 'being a law student'.

I persuaded Sanmeet, who has been teaching Legal Method for some years now, to collaborate with me on updating Learnmore, the legal skills part of Lawbore, in 2012 and this book stems from that partnership. We have written this book in a way we hope will keep you interested; legal skills books can sometimes be quite dense and a bit of a slog to get through, and we wanted to avoid this at all costs.

Lawbore (lawbore.net)

Don't forget to take a look at Lawbore for extra support – the main website has legal events listings, a directory of recommended web resources and a blog around legal careers. The award-winning Learnmore (winner of the Routledge/ALT Teaching Law with Technology Prize 2013) includes videos, talking slideshows and articles focusing around legal skills.

SANMEET

As I sit here with my four-month-old on my lap watching me type and my two-and-a-half-year-old tugging at my leg running off with my computer mouse, I am reminded of the constant need to change how you teach according to your audience. A lecturer's audience needs to feel that their lecturer is credible, can explain and convey ideas and is committed to engaging with them. Every year I teach new students who arrive ready to learn the law. However, what they actually start to learn is not always what they thought they would be learning.

Students often think learning the law will be akin to a legal drama they have watched on the TV and sometimes they even think it is going to be like an American TV drama! I'm not one to shatter dreams but I am tasked with introducing students to the 'real' law. This involves learning the basics like learning what a law report (case) looks like and how to read it, or learning how to find the relevant parts of the law, which can be hidden in a case 50 pages long. This is sometimes a bit of a shock to the system. This part of the job has not changed much but you, the student, have. The heavy reliance on the internet for research, the increased risks of plagiarism resultant from this and the increasing use of e-books, are just some examples of the changes that I have experienced. This all means that I cannot become complacent in my teaching and need to constantly evolve my teaching style to suit the student of the day. This book goes some way in addressing this very point. It is written in a style that we hope most students can relate to, and will assist with the transition from school or college level to university level. It is a book that is far more engaging than most and gives you an honest view from the lecturers. If something is just not a good idea, we make that clear!

My experience of teaching students new to the law extends across a number of subjects including Legal Method, Contract Law and Tort Law and across a number of programmes both undergraduate and postgraduate. As well as running the show on the LLB programme as the Director of the programme, I have been the Director of Moots and the Exams Officer. All of these experiences have poured into this book.

While it is likely that my views may change in a few years' time as I respond to the changing ways in which students learn, I have noted with Emily some of the basic lessons that any law student should learn in this book. Our collective experiences in our various roles have given us a level of insight and knowledge that we have passed on within these pages. Best of luck with your studies and remember some of your lecturers might understand you better than you think as they were students not that long ago – well some of them anyway!

THANKS

We're very grateful to our families for putting up with us, particularly in the latter stages of the writing process. Thanks also to those at Routledge (Fiona Briden and Emily Wells) and Emma Nugent for believing in our slightly quirky ideas from the off, and to Adam Doughty for his brilliant cover illustrations.

Chapter 1
Meet our friends . . .

This book is not intended to be prescriptive in any way; rather it is intended to offer you a helping hand especially in your early years of studying law. You will find that there is not always *one* way to do things or just the *one* answer. For example, you can plan an essay in a number of ways, each method will have its own advantages and disadvantages but your choice will ultimately come down to personal preference and what works for you. You need to explore these things and through trial and error, identify what method is most effective for you personally. You need to be open to trying different techniques in order to be sure that you have found the best fit for you. It is for this reason that we have used examples featuring fictional students to explain ideas and concepts – based not on any particular individuals but who feature a mixture of characteristics we often come across in our teaching. So let's meet them, as they will be popping up throughout this book to explain ideas and work through examples with you.

Meet Ashwin, Brodie, Maisy and Sienna. Here's a quick rundown of what they are like:

SIENNA

Sienna works tirelessly but finds the volume of reading a bit of a struggle. Since she rarely completes the reading for any of her classes, she is not confident in speaking up in tutorials and putting across her ideas. She feels out of her depth constantly. She does however feel more confident in small groups, where she feels she can bounce ideas off other students. Sienna finds it hard enough to keep up with her studies and therefore avoids attending any extra-curricular events as she finds it impossible to squeeze anything extra into her schedule.

MAISY

Maisy is bright and confident but keen to cut corners where possible. She loves to take part in moot competitions, and excels at the advocacy side of this, but limits herself by only reading what is absolutely required.

Similarly for her tutorials she scrapes by on a bare minimum since there are just so many things to read. Maisy likes to find the quickest way to do things and would rather just do 'enough to get by' so she can take part in the social events taking place across the university. Since she does not engage in wider reading, she often finds it hard to concentrate when discussions veer off at a tangent and particular questions are being addressed.

BRODIE

Brodie loves to write about the law, and often contributes to legal blogs and passes comment on tweets and other people's blogs. He often writes essays exceeding the word count as he loves to discuss his personal views

about the status of the law in a given area. Brodie finds undertaking legal research laborious and complicated, always worrying that he has missed something. He isn't keen on preparation and planning, and thinks that it is most important for him to get his ideas down on paper rather than taking time to organise his answers. Brodie does like to attend extra-curricular events since it gives him an opportunity to network and it drives him to get to know more people in the industry.

ASHWIN

Ashwin works very hard in everything that he does, and is super confident. He likes to attend every lecture, tutorial, special talk and everything else in between. It is second nature for him to get involved in tutorials: he contributes a lot and becomes frustrated when others do not participate in discussion as it can become rather one sided.

All four of our friends are entering into a moot competition and need to use the skills in this book to give this competition their best shot. Here is the moot problem that they need to work on and we shall catch up on their progress at the end of each chapter:

IN THE COURT OF APPEAL

Linda Cahill

V

Bulldozer Builders

Linda Cahill decided to have some renovation work carried out on her house. Her friends recommended a company called Bulldozer Builders. Linda invited Bulldozer to quote her for the work that she wanted to have carried out. Bulldozer inspected the building and on account of this inspection, quoted Linda £50,000 for the work. Linda and Bulldozer agreed that the work would start 1 February and if the work was finished by 1 June a bonus of £5,000 would be payable by Linda. Linda explained that it was her daughter's first birthday and she is hosting a big party on 11 June and needs time to set things up for the party. Bulldozer sent over their standard contract to Linda for her signature on the contract, which included the clause about the bonus payment but mistakenly unknown to both parties, the date stated was 10 June rather than 1 June. Linda signed the contract without reading it and did not notice the difference in the date.

Bulldozer duly started the building work and Linda, being so impressed with the standard of their work, asked for a quote to build a garage alongside her house. Bulldozer said that they would add that to their workload and that it would cost £7,000 although they would need this payment upfront to help pay for materials. Linda signed a new contract for the additional building work and happily paid them £7,000 in advance.

Bulldozer finished the renovations by 10 June and started work on the garage. Bulldozer asked Linda for their payment and their bonus payment. Linda refused to pay Bulldozer the bonus on account of them having missed the completion date of 1 June. Bulldozer highlighted that according to the contract that Linda had signed they were entitled to the bonus payment as they had finished their work by 10 June.

When Bulldozer were beginning to dig the foundation for the garage floor, they came across what was discovered to be an unexploded World War II bomb. Bulldozer immediately stopped their work and called the Army bomb disposal team. Bulldozer refused to build the garage as they had already spent £3,000 on materials and it would cost an additional £5,000 to complete due to the days they had lost while waiting for the bomb to be disposed. The result would be that they would be late beginning their next contract with another party and be in breach of that contract.

Linda asked for her £7,000 to be repaid due to a total failure of consideration. Bulldozer refused to pay in accordance with the following clause in their contract:

> 3.1.1 While best endeavours will be made to complete all work, we shall not be liable for any failure of or delay in the performance of this agreement for the period that such failure or delay is due to events beyond our reasonable control, including but not limited to acts of God, war, strikes, government orders or any other *force majeure* event.

The trial judge accepted that in accordance with the principles of offer and acceptance, the relevant date by which the work was to be completed for the bonus to be payable was 10 June and that nothing outside the four corners of the contract could be used to contradict what is contained in the contract as per *L'Estrange v F Graucob Ltd* (1934) 2 KB 394.

The trial judge declined to accept Bulldozer's argument that the discovery of an unexploded World War II bomb frustrated the contract or that its discovery of the bomb falls within the scope of clause 3.1.1 and thus does not invoke the clause. In accordance with *Davis Contractors Ltd v Fareham UDC* [1956] AC 696, mere hardship or inconvenience will not frustrate the contract. In addition, a *force majeure* event must specifically be stated in a *force majeure* clause for it to be effective.

Linda appeals to the Court of Appeal on the first ground:

(i)   That the contract must be interpreted in accordance with the parties true intention which here was that a bonus payment would only be payable if the building work were to be completed by 1 June and the discussion that she had with Bulldozer should be taken into account and the agreement should be rectified to reflect the true intentions of both parties.

Bulldozer cross-appeal to the Court of Appeal on the second ground:

(ii) That the trial judge erred in applying the doctrine of frustration since it is near impossible for Bulldozer's to perform their obligation under the contract and in the alternative, the trial judge interpreted clause 3.1.1 too narrowly as the discovery of the unexploded World War II bomb is an eventuality that falls within the scope of the clause and the contract is therefore frustrated.

Chapter 2

Academic survival skills: standing on your own two feet

2.1 INTRODUCTION

Studying law for the first time is challenging, whether you are coming at it fresh from A-levels or arriving as a graduate of another discipline. There are skills that are very specific to law, and we shall cover many of these throughout this book – you'll see detailed chapters on legal writing, legal research and mooting for example.

There are many skills that are applicable to everyone studying any discipline at university. Often students can discount these, thinking them obvious and wanting to rush onto the 'real' law. This is madness! Knowing how to cope with your workload, manage your time, get the most out of your face-to-face time with lecturers and get better at note-taking are not law-specific, but nevertheless essential. So we'll try and make this as painless as possible.

2.2 LECTURES AND TUTORIALS

For those of you new to university it is a massive shock to the system – going from small classes where you know everyone (might have even been in school with some since pre-school!), to massive lecture theatres seating hundreds of you.

Generally speaking you may be taught both in large groups (via lectures) and small groups (via tutorials, also called seminars). Traditionally the lecture is where you listen to your lecturer telling you all the important stuff about a particular subject – introducing you to key cases and legal principles, as well as raising any areas of uncertainty and perhaps voices of dissent on particular issues. That said, your role won't be a passive one. You will be working on processing, understanding and analysing the information you're listening to. Generally your role as a student is to sit quietly, listen and take notes. For lectures with fewer students (perhaps for elective final year subjects), the format might be a little looser, with more opportunities for student and lecturer interaction.

It is in the smaller group sessions where you get a chance to put what you've learnt in the lectures into practice. Here, you and about 15 others (numbers depending on your university) will get involved in debate and discussion – answering questions, giving presentations and trying out theories.

2.2.1 Teaching mash-ups

Like most walks of life, times are changing, and some lecturers are trying new approaches to make the lectures more engaging. Sitting in a lecture trying to pay attention for an hour or two is challenging for most people. It's not like going to the cinema where you are quite happy to sit and munch popcorn quietly for that period of time. Perhaps with the addition of some visual effects, supporting actors, good jokes, fight scenes, a romantic lead even, we, as lecturers, might be able to keep you glued spellbound to your seats. Alas, glamming up restrictive covenants or proprietary estoppel is a tough call.

Flipped learning is becoming more commonplace – here the large lectures become much more interactive. Students are required to watch or listen to information *before* the lecture – this would be the normal lecture part. Then the time in the lecture is spent in activity – with students working on problems in small groups for example. There might also be quizzes to test your knowledge.

2.2.2 **What do your lecturers want from you?**

Whatever the format our teaching takes, the key thing for us is engagement. We want *you* to play a part – there is nothing more soul-destroying than sitting in a tutorial and NOBODY SPEAKING.

We don't want to lecture again, and we definitely don't want to answer our own questions – gets kind of weird.

We don't mind if you get things wrong – we like helping you learn, but please just contribute.

The tutorial is the *only time* you get to test out that you know what you're talking about. You have an academic right there – so make the most of it. This may be your lecturer, another academic member of staff or a Graduate Teaching Assistant (GTA). Remember that what you cover in this session will be really helpful when it comes to preparing for exams or writing a piece of coursework.

The exemplary student will*:

- read the necessary chapter(s) within the recommended text;
- follow up on any recommended journal articles in the course handout;
- prepare for tutorial thoroughly – answering any questions set, noting anything not sure of to ask in class;
- make notes!;
- add to notes from lecture and tutorial by doing some extra reading – choose a different book, perhaps a monograph or look for some comment online via a practitioner/academic blog or the *Times/ Guardian* law section.

*This won't always be possible – we know sometimes you have coursework deadlines and then that's all you can think about. Sometimes (shock horror!) you have a life outside university and you may have to focus on your family or friends. However try not to get too behind; it is difficult to get back on track. That first year of your law course will absolutely fly by, and then you'll be sat at home trying to work out how to revise in a panic.

2.2.3 The students who drive everyone mad

- The student who says nothing in tutorials – is it just shyness or haven't they done the preparation?
- The student who talks/giggles through lectures.
- The student who monopolises discussions.
- The student who sits in front of their laptop thinking that we don't know that they are more focused on keeping tags on their social media world.

2.3 COMMUNICATING WITH ACADEMICS

So you're at university – you now have lecturers rather than teachers. You will probably have a different lecturer for each subject, and often a different person will take you for tutorial than for the lecture.

You will also have a personal tutor.

We've already mentioned that different modules may be taught in different ways – you may see your lecturer on a weekly or fortnightly basis.

What happens if you're finding something difficult to understand or you've a question about an assessment?

> *Ashwin*:   I just can't get my head around X. I emailed my lecturer but they haven't bothered to reply yet.
>
> *Brodie*:   Yeah that is really difficult; I'm a bit unsure on that too. When did you email them?
>
> *Ashwin*:   Yesterday about 11 pm.
>
> *Brodie*:   Probably a bit soon to expect a reply.

Yes!

It's human nature to think that just because it takes a few seconds to email someone, the reply should be just as speedy. However a few points to note:

1   Your lecturer in a particular subject might have 300+ students in that lecture alone, add to that any other subjects they are responsible for teaching.
2   Your lecturer will also be a personal tutor and may have around 75 students who might need their help.

3   Your lecturer has other commitments outside teaching, these may include:

   (a) *Marking.*
   (b) *Preparation for teaching* (updating materials, designing new modules, keeping up with the latest legal developments).
   (c) *Research* – many of those who teach you will also be researching in preparation for writing new books and journal articles. They may also be putting together applications for getting external funding for their research.
   (d) *University business* – many of your lecturers will also have administrative responsibilities within the law school. This might be in relation to management of mooting, pro bono, assessments or particular programmes. This involves a lot of meetings, as well as the inevitable work resultant from this!
   (e) *Family life* and dare we say it, a love life?

Generally you should only expect a reply within business hours. If you get one outside this – bonus!

All of this means that at peak times in term it wouldn't be unusual for your email to be sat among another 70 received that day in your lecturer's inbox. They will of course reply, but there may be other ways of getting answers.

That's why those tutorials are so important! You have their undivided attention to get clarification, try out your thoughts and get guidance on tricky aspects of that module.

Many universities also lay on extra sessions for those students who are keen for extra support, often run by enthusiastic PhD students. Sign up for these where you can. Other options are to set up informal groups among your friends on the course – you will all have different levels of understanding for different subjects. It makes total sense to pool resources! You are not in competition with each other – use the time to share ideas and form a deeper understanding. This will really help with your motivation.

Your lecturers will also have 'office hours' where they make themselves available to you – sometimes it's more beneficial to book a slot and go through your issue face-to-face, rather than via a long drawn-out email exchange.

2.4 NOTE-TAKING

Cracking when and how you need to take notes is absolutely key to successful study.

First let's consider why we need these notes.

PICTURE THE SCENE ...

(Start of revision period – sun is shining, but the mood is black)

Sienna is sat on her bed sobbing with head in hands, surrounded by files, a laptop, hundreds of pages of scribbled notes.

Everything you do during the year of studying for a particular module is leading up to some kind of an assessment, often in the form of a written piece of coursework and a final exam, although there will be lots of variations on this.

Organisation is dull but so important – if you start out as you mean to go on, the scene above will not feature you! When I speak to undergraduates after their first year, and ask what they'll be changing for Year Two, they always say the way in which they prepare for and recap after taught classes. Their big recognition about that revision period was that they were learning *too much for the first time*.

2.4.1 When will I be taking notes?

The situations will vary but may include some combination of the following:

- while sitting in lectures;
- while preparing for tutorials;
- while participating in tutorials;
- while reading your textbook/casebook;
- while reading case law;
- while reading journal articles or other academic materials.

Everyone's notes are different, and the hardest thing is finding the right level of detail required. You can't write everything down – the point is to pick out the most relevant information, and this takes time to refine.

2.4.2 Lectures

The notes you take in lectures will give you the structure for the rest of your notes. Remember your lecturer can't possibly cover everything there is to know about a subject in the hour or two allotted; you will need to research and find the extra reading yourself.

It would be sensible to use the PowerPoint slides or lecture outline provided by your lecturer as the basis for your notes. You can then just add in any additional details as you follow these along. Do spend *more time listening* than writing though – it is easy to get so carried away writing down everything you hear that you don't have time to reflect on what is actually important in all that content.

2.4.3 Handwritten or typed?

More students use their laptops or tablets to take notes in lectures but there are still some who take notes old-skool style. If you're using a pen and paper then it makes sense to leave lots of spaces under each section so you can add in any notes from additional reading in the relevant spot.

Typing them is obviously much more flexible – you can easily combine lecture, tutorial and additional reading into one document. Try not to get distracted by other things on your laptop though – the lure of Facebook can be hard to resist.

TOP TIP

Always make sure you back up your documents – the number of students whose laptops combust or get stolen each year is significant. Don't take the risk – stick it regularly on a USB or onto a cloud-based storage centre like Dropbox.

2.4.4 Secret code

As you get more practice you'll start to develop your own coding system for notes – using underlining, bold or different colours to indicate key information. Alas for most of us, the merits of Microsoft Word mean you don't get the enjoyment of those special pens with four integral colours.

You could use different colours to signpost different types of information – normal black for the detail from the lecture, another colour for supporting commentary-type material (e.g. passage from the recommended textbook) and yet another for the primary law (the relevant section from a case or piece of legislation).

NOTES EXAMPLE

Juries – banned from taking into account evidence not raised in court – to ensure fair trial & that no convictions occur on the basis of gossip. Contempt of court.

Social media issues

R v Fraill and Sewart (2011)	Juror chatted with a defendant on Facebook re a co-defendant while trial ongoing. Also carried out research while deliberating verdict. Eight months for contempt.
AG v Dallas (2012)	Lecturer researched defendant while a juror on the case, shared findings with other jurors. Given verbal & written warnings about this issue before case began. Six months for contempt.

If you're doing a breakdown of cases, you could use different colours to indicate the case name, legal principle, your own breakdown of the case and any criticism or related authorities.

NOTES EXAMPLE

Objective standard of care: relevant considerations

i   Foreseeability
Was the harm foreseeable or unforeseeable? *Roe v Minster of Health* [1954] 2 QB 66

ii Magnitude of the risk

Likelihood of the harm *Bolton v Stone* [1951] AC 850 and *Miller v Jackson* [1977] QB 96

Severity of the potential damage – seriousness of the consequences *Paris v Stepney Borough Council* [1951] AC 367 and *Harris v Perry* [2008] EWCA Civ 907

iii Practicality of precautions

How practical is it to take precautions to prevent the harm? *Latimer v AEC Ltd* [1953] AC 643 and *Overseas Tankship (UK) Ltd v Miller Steamship Co Pty Ltd, the Wagon Mound* (No 2) [1967] 1 AC 617

iv The utility of defendant's conduct

How worthwhile is the defendant's activity *Watt v Hertfordshire County Council* [1954] 1 WLR 835 and Compensation Act 2006, s 1

v Common practice

Bolitho v City and Hackney HA [1997] 4 All ER 771 and *Sutcliffe v BMI Healthcare* [2007] EWCA Civ 476

Perhaps you could also make a separate file of terms you're not familiar with, so you can check later.

You might make use of different symbols to act as shorthand – alerting you to the significance of certain parts of your notes. You can get creative about these – as long as you know what they mean, that's all that counts! However you might want to use an * or ! to indicate something really important. A ? is always good for when you're not sure on something. Choose a symbol to remind you to check another source for more detail later.

Essentially you can choose the code you employ, just make sure you know what it is and that you are consistent.

Ashwin and Maisy attend their Tort Law lecture – they have different approaches to note-taking. Ashwin is a firm believer in writing everything down; he doesn't want to miss anything. Maisy is keen on cutting down work where possible!

Here's what their notes look like for the same section of the lecture on the *Objective Standard of Care*:

ASHWIN

The objective standard of care

- The question for the court is not what *could* we have expected *this particular defendant* to do in the circumstances?
  - The question must be asked in each situation is *what the reasonable person would have done* in the circumstance.

- Rather the question is: what could we expect a reasonable person to do?
  - The courts apply an objective standard of care – means that D's own view of the reasonableness of his conduct is irrelevant. It also suggests that courts should ignore particular characteristics of D. So if D is a little careless D cannot argue that their standard of care was reasonable since the reasonable person would not usually be careless.

- *Nettleship v Weston* [1971] 2 QB 691
  - It is no defence for a driver to say 'I was a learner-driver under instruction. I was doing my best and could not help it'. Every person driving a car must attain an objective standard measured by the standard of a skilled, experienced and careful driver. That is shown by *McCrone v Riding* [1938] 1 All ER 137, where a learner-driver 'was exercising all the skill and attention to be expected from a person with his short experience', but he knocked down a pedestrian. He was charged with driving 'without due care and attention' contrary to s.12 of the Road Traffic Act 1930; now s.3 (1) of the Road Traffic Act 1960.
  - But what is the standard of care required of the driver? Is it a lower standard than he or she owes towards a pedestrian on the pavement? But, suppose that the driver has never driven a car before, or has taken too much to drink, or has poor eyesight or hearing and, furthermore, that the passenger *knows* it and yet accepts a lift from him. Does that make any difference?
  - Seeing that the law lays down, for all drivers of motor-cars, a standard of care to which all must conform, even a learner driver,

so long as he is the sole driver he must attain the same standard towards all passengers in the car, including an instructor.*

These paragraphs are taken from the judgment itself and need to be referenced so we caution against taking down almost verbatim what the lecturer says as it is often too much detail for your notes and can be written succinctly.

MAISY

The objective standard of care

- What shd partic D have done in the situ?

- **Q**→ What wld reasonable person have done?
    - Objective (obj) standard of care (soc)
    - Not what D thinks but what reasonable person shd have done =obj soc.

- *Nettleship v Weston* [1971] 2 QB 691
    - Learner driver caused accident
    - Soc to be applied?
    - Obj soc makes no difference that D was learner driver
    - Relevant soc = skilled, experienced and careful driver to all relevant people
    - Fair? What if first time driving?

2.4.5 Get visual!

For some, pages and pages of text do not prove as effective as something a little more creative. You can't overestimate the importance of *how* your notes appear on the page. You'll see when we get to the chapter on revision we talk about mind maps in relation to planning question answers, and this has applicability here also. Diagrams, doodles, flowcharts and tables are all vital tools for reinforcing what you've learnt (see Figure 2.1). It's surprising how well a concept gets embedded in your brain when you've changed it from text to something visual – for many students it is often recalled more easily in exams too.

Figure 2.1 Offer and acceptance diagram

2.4.6 Consolidation

Yet another dull word we're afraid!

To avoid that situation we visualised at the beginning of this section, you need to bring it all together. So all your notes on a topic e.g. *psychiatric harm* need to be brought together – so notes from the lecture, tutorial and all extra materials you've read. It makes it much easier in the revision period if this has been done – you can then spend all your time focusing on *getting it in your head*.

2.5 TIME MANAGEMENT

Studying at university is very different to being at school. The onus is on you to manage your time and to manage it well. Once your course gets underway, you will soon remember that there are only 24 hours in a day. There is only so much that you can cram in. You will have competing demands: preparing for tutorials, which involve reading pages and pages, meeting assessment deadlines and potentially preparing for moots. You know that you need to study hard to reap the rewards, but that said, you do not get this time at university again and making friends is also very important indeed. It is true for many of us that the friends that we make at university are friends for life. So how do you fit your studies around your all-important social life, which no doubt also involves regularly updating the world on your activities via social media websites?

You need to make sure that you use your time efficiently and effectively when studying, and learn to balance your commitment to your studies while permitting time for your personal life. It goes without saying that **you** are responsible for your own learning. If you do not put the time in, you will not see the results. Having said that, just because you are studying law does not mean that you should not have a personal life; indeed it is quite the opposite. Your lecturers will encourage you to ensure that you take a couple of evenings off a week from your studies so that you can be refreshed for the next set of classes. So how do you manage your workload?

You need to develop a technique that helps you to take responsibility for your own learning but without burning out, by ensuring that you do have time to do the things that you like as well.

Tip 1
Be honest and think about the way that you study best, as well as what time of day you are at your most productive.

What this really means:

- Think of your university life as a job and work regular working hours between 8 a.m. and 6 p.m.

- Stay back to finish work when you have a lot on. This will help you develop a good work ethic for the real world.

Tip 2
Establish weekly goals that you must meet.

What this really means:

- Set some attainable and clear goals for the week

- Do not set impossible goals because you will end up feeling defeated if you do not meet them. It is better to set small goals ('easy wins') that you realistically think you can meet. This is a great way of boosting your confidence because you know you have achieved your goals for the week

---

Tip 3
Create a study timetable.

What this really means:

- Create a timetable that incorporates your scheduled learning and assessment deadlines so you know exactly what time you have either side of your classes and when you have to submit work. Do not cram in things that you know you cannot feasibly do within a day. It can make you feel like you have failed

- It is true however, that you might draw up a timetable and try it for a week and realise that it needs a few tweaks, it is absolutely fine to go ahead and change it. Remember it is a personal study timetable that works for you, incorporating the way you study and the time it takes you to study. You will learn from your own experience

- Don't feel like you need to be a superstar student and finish everything in record time. Some activities will just take you longer than your friend but equally, you will probably understand some things quicker than your friend

---

Table 2.1 Example timetable

Time slot	Monday	Tuesday	Wednesday	Thursday**	Friday
9–10	Public law lecture	Plan answer for Criminal law coursework	ELS lecture	Prep* Contract law tutorial	Criminal law lecture
10–11		Research for moot competition			
11–12	Research for Criminal law coursework	Contract law lecture	ELS tutorial	Attend careers talk	Prep* Public law tutorial
12–1	Lunch		Lunch	Lunch	
1–2	Criminal law tutorial	Lunch	Commercial awareness group	Gym	Lunch
2–3	Gym	Research for moot competition		Read through and edit Criminal law coursework	Prep* Criminal law tutorial
3–4	Prep* ELS tutorial		Write Criminal law coursework	Pro bono at FRU	Prep* Criminal law tutorial
4–5		Moot club			
5–6	Continue with research for Criminal law coursework	Gym			Get ready for going out

*Prep = preparation for; ** = not a uni day

Table 2.2 What time-management issues do our friends need to consider?

Sienna		Does not need to spend time on Contract law because she gets it but struggles with Public law so needs to incorporate more study time for the extra reading
Ashwin		He needs to spend more time on Tort law because there are so many cases whereas Sienna treats tort law cases like stories, which helps her remember them
Brodie		Does not need to spend time on substantive law but struggles with answering questions, so needs to incorporate practising how to answer questions in his study timetable
Maisy		Keeps missing her own deadlines and relies on staying up way past midnight and energy drinks, which often results in her missing the nine o'clock lectures

Tip 4
Allow time for yourself and your social life.

What this really means:

- Don't go out clubbing every night! Yes it is fun to be away from home and you are finally being treated as an adult. Yet being treated like an adult means that you have to learn how to balance your time. You need to be able to work hard and play hard (as the saying goes . . .)

- A good student is someone who studies hard but is able to put their studies and time at university in perspective by ensuring that they reserve time for their personal and social life. It often makes students better learners since they are able to take a break, refresh and think again about their studies. It's the same as when something seems hard, you stop trying to figure it out, you go away, have a cup of tea, come back to tackle it again and realise that it was not that hard. You just needed to take a break from trying to solve it in one session

- Some students describe the feeling of guilt if they go out instead of studying, but then go on to say that they stay at home looking at their books, getting very little done. The only way around this is to take a break. When you go out, do not feel guilty – you have earned it. When you are at home, study hard – simples! Often taking Friday evenings off and the whole of Saturday off seems to be like a winning formula. (Yes you should study on Sundays!)

Tip 5

Do not leave things to the last minute.

> **What this really means:**
>
> - Finish early or on time
>
> - How many times have you had a deadline and something unexpected came up, which meant that you had to quickly cobble something together that is not your best work, or even that you miss your deadline. Think about university life as your first job in the real world; a senior partner in a firm would not accept poor time-management skills as a reason for you not meeting a deadline. Likewise, you want your tutor to be able to say in a reference: this student is punctual and hands in work in good time, as well as being good at keeping to deadlines
>
> - This leads nicely on to you learning to avoid procrastination . . .

2.6 AVOIDING PROCRASTINATION, AND TIME MANAGEMENT

Have you ever heard the word procrastination? No? Well we are all guilty of it. Think of a time when you know you have a deadline or that you have to get some work done but all you can think about is watching just one more episode of the current box set you are addicted to or playing just one more game on your games console or cleaning your room . . . again! These are examples of procrastination. You want to put off what you really need to do by doing other things, in other words you are just delaying the inevitable. Take the plunge and just do it! Yes it seems hard at first and all you can think of is cleaning your room, because a clear room means a clear mind, but yet you have not built that into your study timetable so what will happen? You will end up missing your own deadlines and possibly your submission deadlines.

2.6.1 What happens when something unexpected happens?

Do not stress! Realistically there will be occasions when something unexpected comes up and this throws you off your study pattern. Do not panic. It is OK. Hopefully all of your good time-management skills mean that you will not be missing any deadlines as you have allowed yourself enough time to complete your work. There may however be the odd occasion when something has come up and you are really up against it. Fear not. Perhaps you have to stay up late to complete your work and this may involve working into the wee small hours of the morning. It is not recommended that you do this often but understandably there are times when this needs to be done.

Reserve these late night study sessions only for when you really need them because otherwise you will struggle in your lectures and tutorials the next day and your notes are not going to be good. Think also about a time when you can catch up with any work that you have not managed to complete. So imagine something unexpected crops up or getting your head around the issues takes longer than expected and you don't manage to complete all of the reading on proprietary estoppel. The best approach is to use your lecture notes and the reading that you can manage to do to get by and make a note that when you next have a reading week or break (not the revision period), that you have to catch up on this topic.

2.6.2 Time management and revision

When it comes to crunch time and you are on study leave to revise, remember these top tips:

- Do not procrastinate.
- Revision means that you should not be learning anything new but rather revising.
- Create a new study timetable for your revision.
- Incorporate breaks and time off into your revision timetable.
- Make sure you schedule time in to practise answering old exam questions under timed conditions.

2.6.3 Time management and coursework

You generally have a few weeks in between being handed an essay title and it needing to be submitted. Once that sinking feeling has passed, it's wise to take a breath and remind yourself of these points:

- *Get started early*: start analysing the question and working out what area you will need to start researching. Grab a couple of books from the library and pore over them until you grasp the relevant area of law.

- *Be methodical*: go through your lecture and tutorial notes to pick out anything relevant.
- *Set aside a few hours to research on the legal databases*: for the finer details, and to read the relevant cases.
- *Don't underestimate how long the writing will take*: it'll be time-consuming to build your argument, incorporate your sources and the various redrafts.
- *Double-check when the deadline is and be ready to submit well in advance of this*: if you're uploading onto your university Virtual learning environment (VLE) there's always a (small) risk that some technical hitch will result in you screaming at your laptop as the deadline passes and the submission box closes.

2.7 WORKING WITH OTHERS

As we mentioned in the earlier section on communicating with academics, it's always beneficial to work with others on your course. This might be in an informal study group, but sometimes you might need to work together formally on an assessment and be graded on your output.

Of course, in the real world you will be likely to find yourself working with others, so getting practice in while at university is important. Many law firm assessment days will incorporate some activity where they can observe how you work with others.

Whether in an informal study group or a group working together towards an assessment, it is vital you set out the steps you'll be taking, a division of workload and some kind of schedule. Without this, you'll just end up chatting about what happened in the latest episode of *Game of Thrones* last night and your precious time will ebb away.

There are various teamwork models out there with clearly defined roles to recognise the fact that individual personality might drive which role you are better at taking on within this scenario. For example, Dr Meredith Belbin identified nine different roles in a team situation – splitting them into action-orientated roles, people-orientated roles and thought-orientated roles. Take a look at his website to see which of those you might best fit in with: www.belbin.com.

Students often feel aggrieved about the prospect of group assessments, particularly if you only get a group mark. The competitive nature of students comes to the fore here as individuals feel like their hard work and intellect is benefitting others, rather than just themselves. Obviously this works both ways and often each member of the group will bring different talents to the task.

Ashwin:	I don't see why we have to do this group assessment. I'd much rather prepare for it on my own.
Maisy:	I know, I bet Sienna won't pull her weight; she's always whispering in lectures and then not contributing in tutorials. She's even late for this first meeting about it. We just get one grade right? Not an individual one each?
Ashwin:	Yes I think so – it's so unfair. I hate the idea that we do all the work and she benefits.
Brodie:	She might be alright – give her a chance. We just need to be organised and make sure everyone has their role and that we set a realistic timetable for work to be done. We'll make sure we all agree on who is doing what, how that task is to be achieved and when it must be completed.
Ashwin:	Hmmm I guess we can give that a go. Not convinced she'll stick to it.
Maisy:	We could perhaps come up with a written team agreement that we all sign? It could state what we commit to individually in terms of meeting attendance, keeping in touch with each other and meeting deadlines.
Brodie:	I like that idea. Like a contract between us?
Ashwin:	Here she comes . . . let's see what happens . . .

However lots can go wrong, particularly if someone doesn't pull their weight, or if personalities clash. With several dominant personalities there is the potential for a power struggle. It's important in these cases to keep pulling the group back to the task at hand. Try to resolve this within the group rather than running straight to your lecturer.

2.8 STAYING IN LOVE WITH LAW

As a student your feelings towards your subject will without a doubt twist and turn – some days you'll be really fired up, others a bit fed up with the deadlines coming out of your ears. There will be modules you are fascinated by, and others that bore you. There will be those you find straightforward and others that seem impenetrable. In the difficult times it is hard to retain enthusiasm, but keeping yourself up to date on what's going on in the world is one way of keeping the flame burning.

Chapter 4 discusses legal research and includes a useful section on how to keep your knowledge current, with tips on useful online resources to help. Another way to keep motivated is to attend events going on in your area – if you're at a London University you are spoilt for choice as many of the events at universities like City University London, LSE and UCL will be open to all. The Institute of Advanced Legal Studies in Russell Square also boasts an amazing number of events throughout the academic year.

You could even start a blog about your experiences – or write occasionally for an existing legal blog (like lawbore.net!). You could write articles about potential law reforms, a case comment on a recent decision, review an event you've been to, interview one of your friends on their recent internship even? There are lots of law essay competitions during the year giving you a chance to flex your writing skills and be in with the chance of some prize money. You can find a long list of these on Learnmore: http://learnmore.lawbore.net/index.php/Law_Essay_Competitions.

Getting involved with a project at your law school or doing some pro bono work will also help keep you enthused about law; you'll feel like you're doing something rewarding towards your future.

CATCHING UP WITH OUR FRIENDS . . .

Ashwin needs to start swotting up on the area that his moot concerns. He finds a textbook on Contract law in the library and begins to make some notes on the relevant areas. Here are his first efforts on *Rectification of Contracts*:

- This is an equitable remedy and therefore discretionary

- It allows for the correction of a mistake in a contract when the true intentions of the parties is not reflected in the contract

- This remedy cannot be used to escape from a bad bargain

- Outcome sought is for the contract to read 1 June not 10 June

- Relevant cases include:

  - *Frederick E. Rose (London) Ltd -v- William H. Pim Jnr. & Co. Ltd* [1953] 2 QB 450 – there is a basic error in what is written but not in what the parties agreed
  - *East v Pantiles (Plant Hire)* (1981) 263 EG 61 – rectification through construction – (i) is there a clear mistake; and (ii) what is the correction sought

- *Chartbrook Ltd v Persimmon Homes Ltd* [2009] 1 AC 1101 – what should be the overall interpretation of the contract in context and the background context can be taken into account to understand the whole matrix of facts.

Can you do any better?

Chapter 3
Your guide to the English legal system: order order

3.1 INTRODUCTION

You have obviously decided to study law for a reason, but now when it comes to it, you need to think about *how* to really study the law and the only way that you can do that is to ask yourself, what is the law about?

The law exists to regulate behaviour. As a society we would like to instil good values and beliefs in all of those around us. But what happens when someone does not follow those values or beliefs? Do we simply say that this person is merely someone to be shunned or do we need to go further and impose some sort of punishment upon them such as a restriction on their liberty or by imposing a fine on them? When do we know which form of punishment to use or indeed if one is suitable at all? It is only by understanding how the law has developed over the years and by questioning the current state of the law that you will start to develop an appreciation of what the law is about and of course how to apply the law. If you do not take the time to think about these issues, you may find that you are lost throughout your studies constantly trying to catch up both with your reading and intellectually. Rather than feel lost, you should feel like you are part of something and therefore try and think about the following:

- How has our legal system developed?
- Who creates the law?
- What are the different sources of law?
- What is the purpose of the different laws?
- What are the different types of law and what are they trying to achieve?
- How do you use the different sources of law?
- How do you interpret the law?
- How do you apply the law?
- Can the law ever be changed?

3.2 HOW HAS OUR LEGAL SYSTEM DEVELOPED?

3.2.1 The common law system

If it is a common law system, does it mean it is not posh?! The common law is the law that is common to all. But that does not take us much further in understanding what it really means. Now for a quick history lesson!

Prior to 1066 when William the Conqueror came into power in England, the law across England was not unified in that different customs or laws prevailed in different areas of the country. Local customs were enforced by the local courts so the law varied across England, meaning that the law of the land was decentralised. William the Conqueror recognised that to unify the country and perhaps some might say to effectively control the country, one central set of laws was needed across the whole country. William the Conqueror, through the help of his aides, reviewed the local customs and laws across the country to decide which ones to incorporate into the central set of laws, which would be common to the land. This ultimately became known as the common law.

In terms of how the common law system developed, prior to the Common Law Procedure Acts of 1852 and 1854, it operated on the basis of what is referred to as the rigid writ system. A right only existed if there was a procedure to enforce it.

That is to say, the form was considered, rather than the substance of the claim, i.e. the substance of the claim could have been perfectly worthy of being heard in court but if an appropriate writ did not exist, it could not be taken any further. This was problematic largely because the claim could be a good one but could not proceed any further. Where is the justice in such a system that places such importance on the form and not the actual substance of the claim? Wouldn't you be frustrated if you had a good case to put forward but were stopped because it did not fit into a category that that officials were familiar with? Seems rather unfair doesn't it? Claimants with a good claim but without the procedure to enforce it would be left without recourse to the courts and therefore left without remedy. The common law was overly strict. You can now understand why it is referred to as the 'rigid' writ system.

3.2.2 Equity

The common law was not initially then perceived as flexible as it is today and was just too rigid to achieve effective justice. Something else was needed to help ease the rigidity in the system. As a result, a parallel system of rules developed under the umbrella of equity. Those who suffered through the writ system would petition the King to exercise his prerogative power in their favour. In other words, they would ask the King to make an exception for their case. The King, and later the Lord Chancellor, would deal with such petitions by referring them to the King's Council and other justices. The Lord Chancellor was also known as the keeper of the King's conscience and carried out administrative and judicial tasks on behalf of the King. The Lord Chancellor was also the head of the Court of Chancery, which issued the writs in the first place. It then made sense that the Lord Chancellor oversaw exercise of any discretion when dealing with such petitions. However, the petitions to the King became so numerous that this became a body of law in its own right known as equity. Equity essentially means fairness and justice.

Some examples of equitable maxims are shown on the facing page.

So the state of affairs was that there were two parallel systems at work; one was the common law system through the writ system, and the other was the equitable system. The two legal systems were at work side by side, each with their own courts, procedures, remedies and routes of appeal.

EXAMPLES OF EQUITABLE MAXIMS

- *He who comes to equity must come with clean hands* – in other words if you have behaved in manner that is unconscionable, then you cannot expect to avail yourself using equity.
- *Delay defeats equity* – in other words, if you delay unreasonably in bringing a claim, equitable remedies may not be available to you.
- *Equity will not suffer a wrong without a remedy* – in other words the party that is wronged may ask for an appropriate remedy, which may not be monetary in nature, for example, an injunction.

3.2.3 Common law v equity

As is often the case, when there are two competing systems at work, there will be scope for conflict and only one can win. Where there was a conflict between the common law and equity, it was decided in *Earl of Oxford's Case* (1615) 1 Rep Ch 1 that given that equity is about fairness and justice, equity will always prevail and govern the situation.

Recognising the problems with the writ system, and given the way the common law and equity systems had developed, change was needed. The rigid writ system was eventually abolished by the Common Law Procedure Acts of 1852 and 1854. The effect of these statutes is that the law will instead consider the substance of the claim rather than the form or procedure for enforcing the right. It was also determined that rather than having two different legal systems, the two should fuse. This fusion was brought about by the Judicature Acts of 1873 and 1875.

The Judicature Acts led to the joining together of the two systems so that now all courts can apply both the common law and equity. Note though that there are still two forms of law but they are administered in the same legal system. You might say that there has been a fusion of *administration* of the rules rather than a fusion of the rules.

There ends the history lesson!

3.3 COMMON V CIVIL SYSTEM OF LAW

Now that you have understood how our legal system has developed, you may be wondering where you can find the law. You would be right to think about this.

A unique feature of the common law is that it is not written down in one place, in that it is an uncodified system. You have various places where you can find it, such as statutes and cases. Judges therefore have a strong hand in shaping the law of the country in a common law system. Compare this with the legal systems on the continent, which are known as civil legal systems where the law, both substantive and procedural, is codified and can be found in a single civil code. The key differences between a common law and civil law system are that the common law system operates on an adversarial basis whereas a civil system operates on an inquisitorial basis. In an adversarial approach, both sides of the case, i.e. the claimant or prosecution and the defendant argue their case before the judge and the judge acts as referee. Think of a US television drama that you may have seen where one party raises an objection before a judge and you will soon get the idea of an adversarial system. Compare this with a civil law system, which usually operates using an inquisitorial approach. This involves the judge making a decision by applying the relevant civil code, which enables them to inquire and ascertain what the relevant facts in the case are. Judges in a civil law system do not therefore have such a strong hand in shaping the law of the country.

The way in which a country has developed has determined whether it has adopted a common law system or a civil law system. Each appears to be appropriate for the country's constitutional set up and each has its advantages and disadvantages. For example, in a country with a common law system there is flexibility because the law is not written down in a strict code, whereas in a civil legal system there is little scope to take a broad interpretation of the law because it is written down. Having said that, one may argue that there is greater certainty in a civil legal system precisely *because* the law can be found in a civil code, whereas it cannot be found in one place in a common law system, which relies on being able to decipher what the precise law is in each case.

3.4 WHO CREATES THE LAW AND WHAT ARE THE DIFFERENT SOURCES OF LAW?

The primary law of this country comes from legislation and case law. Who creates either of these and why are these so important? Not all areas of law will be covered by legislation and may instead be covered by case law. Some decisions in cases are deemed to be so important that legislation may be passed on the same matter to give effect to political will and give the issue greater recognition and certainty. Such legislation will then be interpreted and understood using the cases on which is based.

Different areas of the law depend on legislation and case law in varying quantities and this is because they have different functions to perform.

3.4.1 Public v private

Public law is said to rule the nature of the relationship between the individual (e.g. you) and the state (England and Wales).

Private law governs the relationship between individuals or private organisations.

Thinking about the modules you might study or areas of legal practice – Constitutional law, Human Rights and Criminal law fall within the public sphere and Contract, Tort, Land and Equity within the scope of private law. Commercial law has some elements of both, as does EU law, which concerns relationships both between individuals and between states.

3.4.2 Civil v criminal

Criminal law falls within the public sphere because that law sets out how reasonable people should behave and the boundaries in which they operate. Anyone stepping outside this is said to have committed an offence against the whole of society, and sanctions must be applied.

Civil law on the other hand, kicks in when issues arise between individuals (e.g. neighbours arguing over trees growing too tall) or between an individual and a business (e.g. damage done to a dress at a dry cleaner), or between businesses (e.g., dispute over the right to use a particular brand name).

Civil cases are brought in the County Court, with those where the money involved is more significant or the issues complex commencing at the High Court. Criminal cases kick off at the Magistrates' Court, with indictable offences (the most serious) going straight to the Crown Court. Appeals follow different routes but can go to the Court of Appeal and Supreme Court.

There are further differences between civil and criminal law in relation to terminology – those accused of a criminal offence are called 'defendants', while those bringing the case in a civil action are called 'claimants'.

Differences are also present in relation to how the case has to be proved and where the burden lies. In criminal law the burden of proof is high – the prosecution (the Crown Prosecution Service) have to prove beyond reasonable doubt that the defendant is guilty of the offence. We hear many celebrities accused of criminal offences in the press talking of how they will fight to prove their innocence, but it is not for the defendant to prove this, *although of course this helps!*

In civil actions the claimant must prove their case on the 'balance of probabilities'. This basically means more likely than not – a much lower burden of proof than in the criminal courts.

The possible outcomes are also different – in a criminal court it is conviction (found guilty) or acquittal (found not guilty). Conviction will lead to sentencing for a stint in prison, a fine or a community service order. In the civil court, the claimant is looking for a remedy, usually monetary but it can sometimes be an injunction (stopping the defendant from doing something).

3.4.3 European law

Then there is law that comes from the European Union. This too is a source of law and is divided into two areas, primary and secondary. Primary EU law is generally the law contained in the various EU treaties whereas secondary EU law consists of regulations, directives and decisions delivered by the Court of Justice of the European Union. There are three main institutions based in Brussels. There is the European Commission, which represents the interests of the EU as a whole, the Council of the European Union, which represents the interests of the Member States, and the European Parliament, which represents the interests of EU citizens. The Court of Justice of the European Union is however based in Luxembourg. Confusingly, there is also the European Council, which is an institution that comprises the heads of each Member State, which usually meets around four times a year to set the overall agenda of the EU. Phew! You can take a quick breather now – you will need it!

OK, so how does EU law fit into UK law? EU law imposes obligations but also gives rights to EU citizens and businesses in all of its Member States. Member States is the term used to refer to the countries that have joined the EU. There are currently 28 Member States including the UK, which joined the EU in 1973. The UK and all other Member States for that matter need to ensure that all relevant EU law is accessible at national level. This is to say, citizens will want to be able to understand how the law applies in their country and their legal system. So each Member State is tasked with implementing EU law at national level (this is also referred to as domestic level). Citizens of the EU can then go to their national courts and enforce their EU law rights as opposed to having to go the Court of Justice of the European Union.

The thing to get your head around is that EU law is not above or below national law, but rather it sits alongside it at the top level. Both sources of law are supreme in their own right. So EU law is influential in that it does not bind the UK but the UK must have regard to it.

3.4.4 Human rights law

Ever heard someone say: 'but that's my human right to . . .'? Well there are some rights that are considered to be so very important that they should never be compromised. We are not talking about your right to have a lie in until the afternoon on a Saturday to nurse your hangover, but rather we are talking about the important stuff, which is sometimes taken for granted. So for example, the right to life, the right not to be tortured, the right to have a fair trial or the right to have a private and family life. These, as well as some other rights, are deemed to be so important that a convention was created after the atrocious events of both World Wars called the European Convention on Human Rights (ECHR) in order to recognise the rights to which all human beings should be entitled. This was a real turning point in making the world aware that these important rights must be protected for not to do so is inhumane.

A word of warning here, this is unrelated to the EU or the Court of Justice of the European Union. The institution that drafted the Convention is known as the Council of Europe and there is a separate court called the European Court of Human Rights, which hears cases concerning violations of human rights and is based in Strasbourg. Those countries that have signed up to the

Convention/Council are called Member States. Remember though these countries may or may not be in the European Union! Some countries are members of both; some are not. That said, the EU will usually require its Member States to adhere to the rights contained in the Convention. Now go and take another breather!

Again, how does human rights law fit into UK law? Since the UK has signed up to the ECHR, it has to implement the rights contained within it at national level. The UK does this through the Human Rights Act 1998. But wait a minute; why not just rely on the ECHR itself? Why do we need yet more law to say the same thing? Taking a case to the European Court of Human Rights in Strasbourg is an expensive business, not to mention time-consuming, so having law that broadly implements the rights contained in the ECHR helps UK citizens to get a better sense of what their Convention rights are and of course it means that they can apply the law in their national courts without the need to go to Strasbourg.

Both strands of law are supreme in their own right but in terms of their relationship, English courts will, as far as possible, interpret the law in a way that is compatible with the law contained in the ECHR and jurisprudence from the European Court of Human Rights will be considered.

This is an obligation that is set out in s 2 of the Human Rights Act 1998:

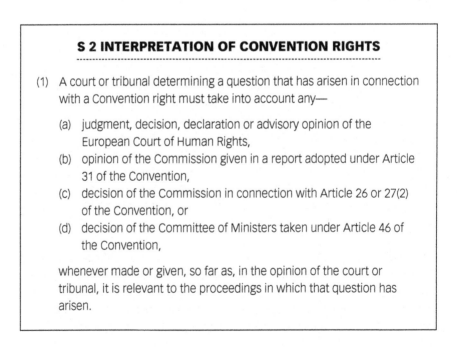

S 2 INTERPRETATION OF CONVENTION RIGHTS

(1) A court or tribunal determining a question that has arisen in connection with a Convention right must take into account any—

   (a) judgment, decision, declaration or advisory opinion of the European Court of Human Rights,
   (b) opinion of the Commission given in a report adopted under Article 31 of the Convention,
   (c) decision of the Commission in connection with Article 26 or 27(2) of the Convention, or
   (d) decision of the Committee of Ministers taken under Article 46 of the Convention,

   whenever made or given, so far as, in the opinion of the court or tribunal, it is relevant to the proceedings in which that question has arisen.

There may, however, be occasions where English law is not compatible with a provision contained in the ECHR in which case the English court may make a declaration of incompatibility. This option is set out in s 4 of the Human Rights Act 1998:

S 4 DECLARATION OF INCOMPATIBILITY

(1)   Subsection (2) applies in any proceedings in which a court determines whether a provision of primary legislation is compatible with a Convention right.

(2)   If the court is satisfied that the provision is incompatible with a Convention right, it may make a declaration of that incompatibility.

(3)   Subsection (4) applies in any proceedings in which a court determines whether a provision of subordinate legislation, made in the exercise of a power conferred by primary legislation, is compatible with a Convention right.

(4)   If the court is satisfied—

    (a)   that the provision is incompatible with a Convention right, and

    (b)   that (disregarding any possibility of revocation) the primary legislation concerned prevents removal of the incompatibility,

it may make a declaration of that incompatibility.

3.5 SOURCES OF LAW

There are two principal sources of law. These are primary and secondary sources of law. Pay attention here because we shall keep coming back to this distinction especially when discussing legal research.

Primary sources are the real deal. These are the sources from which most secondary sources derive. Legislation and cases are primary sources of law. Take for example, the casebooks that you have been told to buy; they usually contain a short excerpt of a law report together with the author's interpretation or comment on the case. But is someone else's interpretation better than yours? What could be better than reading the case itself and coming up with your own interpretation of the case? This is why it is so important for you to understand the distinction. Do you want to use something that someone else has interpreted or do you want to provide your own interpretation of the law?

Often this will come down to a question of confidence. Do you feel confident enough to read a case or legislation for yourself and apply it or do you need to read someone else's view to make sure that you are on the right lines before you apply it? Most of us use both approaches. We might read some commentary of the case before we read the case in full or read some notes on a piece of legislation because it helps us to stay on track. This is why *both* primary and secondary sources are so valuable. Just because a source falls within the category of a secondary source, that does not mean that it should be afforded secondary status.

Secondary sources include books (which we talk about in detail within Chapter 4), journals, encyclopedias, digests, dictionaries and official publications from Parliament or organisations like the Law Commission. On top of this are sources like newspapers, websites, blogs and reports from other organisations. Secondary sources can also assist in formulating that 'critical analysis' you so often see mentioned in marking schemes. This is going that one step further from merely describing the law – it is where you actually start to compare and contrast, tease out inconsistencies and missing logic, where you form your opinions informed by the commentary of others. This is where we get essays into high 2:1/first level marks.

So let's now turn our attention to whether a source is primary or secondary, what each source of law really means and how to use them.

3.6 LEGISLATION: PRIMARY SOURCE

The government of the day will have some ideas that fit into their political agenda about what they would like to change to improve the country. The government does not want to remove existing laws and replace them with laws that fit in with their agenda, but rather want to enhance the existing legal system through creating some new laws that they believe will help the country and through creating laws that take into account world affairs including the UK's commitment to the EU.

The government will bring about new laws by putting forward proposals on which it will seek comments that may be received in the form of a Green and/or White Paper (a White Paper is a stronger statement on the matter). After having received comments on these proposals, they will be debated and consulted on in cabinet committees and approved by the committee, then the relevant ministers responsible for championing the proposals will convert them into Bills.

The Houses of Parliament consider the Bills put forward with a view to them becoming law. These Bills must be approved and agreed upon by both the House of Commons and House of Lords. If they are agreed and approved, the Queen will be asked to give her Royal Assent to the Bills. Once received, the Bills will become Acts of Parliament.

Take a look at Figure 3.1, which shows an example of an Act and how to read it.

We have said that it is easier to use statutes because the law is written down in a structured way whereas in cases you need to search for the legal reasoning, it is nonetheless a particular skill of a lawyer to be able to decipher an Act of Parliament and understand what it really means. The placement of a comma, for example, can change the meaning of a particular provision and a lawyer should be able to understand the significance of such a comma. This is also an opportunity for a lawyer to put forward a creative interpretation of a provision so that it can be considered in support of their argument. Equally though, lawyers should be able to anticipate how it may be interpreted so as to defeat their argument. This is part of your journey in learning how to critically analyse text. It will become your task to convey the precise meaning of a statute to others and identify meanings the non-lawyer cannot.

To help you in your endeavour to read and understand a statute, use the information readily available to you in the statute itself. So look for the following:

(i)   *Preamble* – older statutes usually contain a preamble so if there is not one, refer to the long title instead.
(ii) *Short title* – this is the normal and quickest way to refer to a statute.
(iii) *Long title* – this explains the purpose of the Act.
(iv) *Definitions section* – they help give meaning to words in relevant context.
(v)   *Objectives section* – if there is one.
(vi) *Headings* – these signpost different sections of the statute.
(vii) *Schedules* – if there are some, as they add specific detail.
(viii) *Margin notes and/or headings* – these are useful to guide you.
(ix) *Explanatory notes* – these can be found in more recent statutes.

There are also other tools that you can use to understand an Act. Sometimes there are explanatory notes available for when the Act was being debated when it was merely a Bill. In a similar vein following the decision in *Pepper (Inspector of Taxes) v Hart* [1993] HL, it is also possible to refer to Hansard for further guidance on how a statute should be interpreted. Some secondary sources, which are discussed later in this chapter, may also be of help when trying to interpret statutes.

Unfair Contract Terms Act 1977 — Short Title

1977 CHAPTER 50 — Citation

An Act to impose further limits on the extent to which under the law of England and Wales and Northern Ireland civil liability for breach of contract, or for negligence or other breach of duty, can be avoided by means of contract terms and otherwise, and under the law of Scotland civil liability can be avoided by means of contract terms. — Long Title

[26th October 1977] — Date of Royal Assent

BE IT ENACTEDby the authority of the same, as follows:— — Enacting Formula

Part I Amendment of Law for England and Wales and Northern Ireland

Introductory

1Scope of Part I

(1)For the purposes of this Part of this Act, " negligence " means the breach—
(a)of any obligation, arising from the express or implied terms of a contract, to take reasonable care or exercise reasonable skill in the performance of the contract;
(b)of any common law duty to take reasonable care or exercise reasonable skill (but not any stricter duty);
(c)of the common duty of care imposed by the Occupiers' Liability Act 1957 or the Occupiers' Liability Act (Northern Ireland) 1957.
(2)This Part of this Act is subject to Part III; and in relation to contracts, the operation of sections 2 to 4 and 7 is subject to the exceptions made by Schedule 1.
(3)In the case of both contract and tort, sections 2 to 7 apply (except where the contrary is stated in section 6(4)) only to business liability, that is liability for breach of obligations or duties arising—
(a)from things done or to be done by a person in the course of a business (whether his own business or another's); or
(b)from the occupation of premises used for business purposes of the occupier;
and references to liability are to be read accordingly.
(4)In relation to any breach of duty or obligation, it is immaterial for any purpose of this Part of this Act whether the breach was inadvertent or intentional, or whether liability for it arises directly or vicariously.
Avoidance of liability for negligence, breach of contract, etc.

2Negligence liability — Headings
(1)A person cannot by reference to any contract term or to a notice given to persons generally or to particular persons exclude or restrict his liability for death or personal injury resulting from negligence.
(2)In the case of other loss or damage, a person cannot so exclude or restrict his liability for negligence except in so far as the term or notice satisfies the requirement of reasonableness.
(3)Where a contract term or notice purports to exclude or restrict liability for negligence a person's agreement to or awareness of it is not of itself to be taken as indicating his voluntary acceptance of any risk.

3Liability arising in contract — Main Body
(1)This section applies as between contracting parties where one of them deals as consumer or on the other's written standard terms of business.
(2)As against that party, the other cannot by reference to any contract term—
(a)when himself in breach of contract, exclude or restrict any liability of his in respect of the breach; or
(b)claim to be entitled—
(i)to render a contractual performance substantially different from that which was reasonably expected of him, or

Figure 3.1 Example of an Act of Parliament

(ii)in respect of the whole or any part of his contractual obligation, to render no performance at all,

except in so far as (in any of the cases mentioned above in this subsection) the contract term satisfies the requirement of reasonableness.

...

[Main Body]

Schedules

[Schedules]

Schedule 1 SCOPE OF SECTIONS 2 TO 4 AND 7

1 Sections 2 to 4 of this Act do not extend to—

(a)any contract of insurance (including a contract to pay an annuity on human life);

(b)any contract so far as it relates to the creation or transfer of an interest in land, or to the termination of such an interest, whether by extinction, merger, surrender, forfeiture or otherwise;

(c)any contract so far as it relates to the creation or transfer of a right or interest in any patent, trade mark, copyright, registered design, technical or commercial information or other intellectual property, or relates to the termination of any such right or interest;

(d)any contract so far as it relates—

(i)to the formation or dissolution of a company (which means any body corporate or unincorporated association and includes a partnership), or

(ii)to its constitution or the rights or obligations of its corporators or members;

(e)any contract so far as it relates to the creation or transfer of securities or of any right or interest in securities.

2 Section 2(1) extends to—

(a)any contract of marine salvage or towage;

(b)any charterparty of a ship or hovercraft; and

(c)any contract for the carriage of goods by ship or hovercraft;

but subject to this sections 2 to 4 and 7 do not extend to any such contract except in favour of a person dealing as consumer.

Figure 3.1 continued

In particular though, there are some rules of interpretation that are employed to interpret statutes but they are to be used as blunt tools or broad approaches. One or the other may be used. There is not a particular rule that is used in any given circumstance.

3.6.1 Statutory interpretation

3.6.1.1 The literal rule

This rule is perhaps the easiest to explain, as it is self-explanatory. The literal and ordinary meaning of the words should be used. If the words of the statute are clear then the ordinary meaning of the words should be used as the most appropriate way to give effect to the intention of Parliament. If the use of the literal rule were to lead to absurd or inconsistent results the literal rule would not be used.

EXAMPLE OF THE LITERAL RULE

Fisher v Bell [1961] 1 QB 394

This is a good example to use since you will no doubt come across it in your early studies of Contract law. This case concerned a shopkeeper who displayed a flick knife in his shop window with a ticket behind it bearing the words 'Ejector knife – 4s'. Section 1 (1) of the Restriction of Offensive Weapons Act 1959 stated the following:

Penalties for offences in connection with dangerous weapons:

(1) Any person who manufactures, sells or hires or offers for sale or hire, or exposes or has in his possession for the purpose of sale or hire or lends or gives to any other person—

    (a) any knife which has a blade which opens automatically by hand pressure applied to a button, spring or other device in or attached to the handle of the knife, sometimes known as a 'flick knife' or 'flick gun'; or

    (b) any knife which has a blade which is released from the handle or sheath thereof by the force of gravity or the application of centrifugal force and which, when released, is locked in place by

---

> means of a button, spring, lever, or other device, sometimes known as a 'gravity knife',
>
> shall be guilty of an offence and shall be liable on summary conviction in the case of a first offence to imprisonment for a term not exceeding three months or to a fine not exceeding fifty pounds level 4 on the standard scale or to both such imprisonment and fine, and in the case of a second or subsequent offence to imprisonment for a term not exceeding six months or to a fine not exceeding two hundred pounds level 4 on the standard scale or to both such imprisonment and fine.

The police alleged that the shopkeeper had offered the knife for sale contrary to s 1. It was held that the shopkeeper had committed no such offence since he had not offered the knife for sale. At most, he was asking customers to make invitations to treat. You will learn early on in contract law the importance of the distinction between an offer and an invitation to treat and that usually a display of goods in a shop is considered to be an invitation to treat. Section 1 of the 1959 Act does not refer to invitations to treat and therefore the shopkeeper had not committed an offence. If Parliament intended to bring this situation within the ambit of the Act, then it should have included a precise definition of offer for sale, which covered this type of situation.

THINKING POINT

What words should Parliament have used in section 1 (1) of the Restriction of Offensive Weapons Act 1959 to cover the situation that arose in *Fisher v Bell*?

3.6.1.2 The golden rule

This rule requires words to be read in their plain and ordinary way but if that leads to an absurd result then the words must be read in the context of the provision. This then gives the courts some latitude in interpreting a statute in order to give effect to Parliament's intention.

EXAMPLE OF THE GOLDEN RULE

Take the decision of *R v Allen (Henry)* (1872) LR 1 CCR 367, which is a classic example often used to demonstrate the operation of this rule. The defendant married Sarah Cunningham, who died in August 1866, leaving a niece named Harriet Crouch. On 30 November 1867, he married Ann Pearson Gutteridge, and on 2 December 1871, while Ann Pearson Gutteridge was still alive he married the niece of his former wife, Harriet Crouch! The central question in this case was whether this constituted bigamy according to s 57 of the Offences against the Persons Act 1861 which stated the following:

S 57 Bigamy. Offence may be dealt with where offender shall be apprehended. Not to extend to second marriages, etc. herein stated.

> Whosoever, being married, shall marry any other person during the life of the former husband or wife, whether the second marriage shall have taken place in England or Ireland or elsewhere, shall be guilty of felony, and being convicted thereof shall be liable . . . to be kept in penal servitude for any term not exceeding seven years . . .

> Provided, that nothing in this section contained shall extend to any second marriage contracted elsewhere than in England and Ireland by any other than a subject of Her Majesty, or to any person marrying a second time whose husband or wife shall have been continually absent from such person for the space of seven years then last past, and shall not have been known by such person to be living within that time, or shall extend to any person who, at the time of such second marriage, shall have been divorced from the bond of the first marriage, or to any person whose former marriage shall have been declared void by the sentence of any court of competent jurisdiction.

Read literally s 57 would lead to an absurd result in that if the word 'marry' were to be interpreted literally, no one could be guilty of the offence. Parliament obviously was referring to a person who went through the ceremony of a marriage rather than someone who literally marries another.

ACTIVITY

A asks B for a 'lift'. Should B:

(a)   physically 'lift' A off the ground (absurd); or

(b)   offer A a 'lift' in his car (ordinary and plain meaning)?

3.6.1.3 The mischief rule

Here the courts will look at the precise mischief or wrong that Parliament sought to target in the statute and thus interpret the statute with that in mind. This rule requires the courts to consider the previous law in order to understand Parliament's intention.

There are four questions that the courts must ask according to *Heydon's Case* (1584) 3 Co Rep 7a:

(i)   What was the common law before the making of the Act?
(ii)   What was the mischief and defect for which the common law did not provide?
(iii)   What remedy did Parliament intend to provide?
(iv)   What was the true reason for that remedy?

The issue with this rule of course is that the courts must be in a position to know what precise mischief Parliament intended to target. The courts could use the preamble of the Act to decipher this but nowadays a preamble is not always provided. There is of course also the assumption here that there is only one mischief that is addressed by the provision.

EXAMPLE OF THE MISCHIEF RULE

Smith v Hughes [1960] 1 WLR 830 is another titillating example, which you will not easily forget!

This case concerned two prostitutes who would stand on a balcony or behind windows in their house, and gain the attention of men passing in the street by tapping on the balcony rail or window pane and inviting them into their house. The Street Offences Act 1959 s 1 stated the following:

> S 1 It shall be an offence for a common prostitute to loiter or solicit in a street or public place for the purposes of prostitution.

The prostitutes of course were not soliciting in a *street* or a *public place* but rather their balconies or behind their windows. Neither the balcony nor window could be construed as part of a street. It was therefore argued by the defendants that their actions did not fall within the ambit of s 1.

Using the mischief rule, it was held by the court that s 1 did not specify that the person who is doing the soliciting must be in the street in that as long as one of the parties involved is in the street, that would suffice to bring the section into play. The mischief aimed at by this Act was to 'clean up the streets' and interpreting the section in this way would allow for that objective to be met.

ACTIVITY

A is the student representative for his year. He notices that some students are posting inappropriate comments about a lecturer on a popular social media website. He emails his fellow students along the following lines:

> If any student posts inappropriate comments about any of their lecturers on a social media website in contravention of the university student charter, they will be referred to an academic misconduct panel.

A then notices a handwritten note on the school noticeboard, which contains inappropriate comments about a lecturer. The note is signed by B with a smiley face.

Can A refer B to an academic misconduct panel?

3.6.1.4 The purposive approach

This approach involves the courts considering the purpose for which the legislation has been drafted and interpreting the provision with that in mind. This is arguably the most sensible approach of them all since the courts will strive to give effect to Parliament's intention by looking beyond the four corners of the statute to meet the objective that Parliament intended. There is of course a risk with this approach. How much latitude do the courts have in forming their interpretation? Could the courts go beyond what Parliament intended?

EXAMPLE OF THE PURPOSIVE APPROACH

R v S of S for Health ex parte Quintavalle (on behalf of Pro-Life Alliance) [2003] 2 WLR 692

This case asked the question whether live human embryos created by cell nuclear replacement (CNR) fall outside the regulatory scope of the Human Fertilisation and Embryology Act 1990 and whether licensing the creation of such embryos is prohibited by section 3(3)(d) of that Act. The argument raised by Pro-Life Alliance was that since embryos created by CNR are not fertilised as set out in s 1 of the 1990 Act, their activities fell outside the scope of the Act.

Human Fertilisation and Embryology Act 1990

1   Meaning of 'embryo', 'gamete' and associated expressions.

(1)   In this Act, except where otherwise stated—

    (a)   embryo means a live human embryo where fertilisation is complete, and

    (b)   references to an embryo include an egg in the process of fertilisation, and, for this purpose, fertilisation is not complete until the appearance of a two cell zygote.

The issue here was that this Act referred to embryos that are fertilised, but the embryos created by CNR are not fertilised. It was held by the House of Lords that the purposive approach should be adopted in such circumstances and the purpose for which Parliament drafted this Act was to regulate the use of human embryos.

This is also an example of when explanatory notes can come in handy to understand Parliament's intention (see discussion above at 3.6 'Legislation: primary source'). The explanatory notes state that the Act regulates the creation, keeping and use of embryos outside the human body and the storage and use of gametes to create embryos. From this the purpose of the Act can be deduced, namely to regulate the practices using human embryos.

The use of the purposive approach of the House of Lords is summed up quite succinctly by Lord Bingham ([2003] 2 AC 687, 695):

> The basic task of the court is to ascertain and give effect to the true meaning of what Parliament has said in the enactment to be construed. But that is not to say that attention should be confined and a literal interpretation given to the particular provisions which give rise to difficulty. Such an approach not only encourages immense prolixity in drafting, since the draftsman will feel obliged to provide expressly for every contingency which may possibly arise. It may also (under the banner of loyalty to the will of Parliament) lead to the frustration of that will, because undue concentration on the minutiae of the enactment may lead the court to neglect the purpose which Parliament intended to achieve when it enacted the statute. Every statute other than a pure consolidating statute is, after all, enacted to make some change, or address some problem, or remove some blemish, or effect some improvement in the national life. The court's task, within the permissible bounds of interpretation, is to give effect to Parliament's purpose. So the controversial provisions should be read in the context of the statute as a whole, and the statute as a whole should be read in the historical context of the situation which led to its enactment.

ACTIVITY

In order to curb potential for cheating in examinations, the university student charter states that it is a breach of exam regulations to use a mobile phone in an exam room.

Student A is caught using his smart watch in the exam room when taking his Contract law exam.

Is this an offence in accordance with the student charter?

3.7 CASE LAW: PRIMARY SOURCE

You will hear the term common law used in a number of ways and it may be used in a way that does not describe the legal system but rather the source of law. The term common law can refer to the use of case law.

Aside from legislation, another way of law being made is through the court system whereby a court makes a decision and if the court is high enough in the hierarchy, the decision will be said to have created a precedent, which will be binding on all courts below it (see below 3.7.4 'The doctrine of judicial precedent'). So a decision in a case can be binding. We shall go onto explore which part of the decision is binding shortly.

The first thing that any student needs to get to grips with is what a case looks like. Figure 3.2 on the following page shows an example of a case that you will soon become familiar with in Contract law.

3.7.1 Law reports

Preparation for any tutorial will require you to look in detail at cases.

A few basic facts:

1   Cases are found within law reports.
2   Law reports are volumes of cases.
3   There are over 100 different series of law reports in the UK alone, published by a selection of publishing companies.

Once upon a time (pre-1865) there were barristers who, when not tied up with advocacy, sat in court and wrote up or 'reported' on other cases. They published them in slim volumes, imaginatively named after themselves. These are now commonly known as the 'nominate reports'.

Frustratingly for a common law jurisdiction, what this meant was that the common law was held within many separate volumes, with very mixed quality and accuracy. Aside from this, the lack of any overarching organisational body meant it was difficult to find a case unless you knew who the law reporter was. Nightmare! Note that many of the cases reported in the nominate reports were later reprinted in the English Reports, complete with index.

26 — Page number

[1962] 2 QB — Case citation

HONGKONG FIR SHIPPING CO. LTD. v. KAWASAKI KISEN KAISHA LTD.

[QUEEN'S BANK DIVISION AND COURT OF APPEAL] — Court

HONGKONG FIR SHIPPING CO. LTD. *v.* KAWASAKI KISEN KAISHA LTD. — Case name

[1957 H. No. 2571.]

1961 Jan. 30, 31;
Feb. 1, 2, 3, 6, 7, 8, 9, 10, 13, 14, 15, 16, 17, 22.

Salmon J. — Judge

C. A.

1961 Oct. 30, 31;
Nov. 1, 2, 6; — Date and hearing of judgment
Dec. 20.

Shipping — Charterparty — Seaworthiness — Condition precedent, whether — Time charter — Vessel unseaworthy by reason of inadequate engine room staff — Breakdowns and delays — Vessel off hire for 5 out of 13½ weeks — Further 15 weeks required for repairs — Whether charterers entitled to rescind — Whether charter frustrated.

Contract — Condition or warranty — Intermediate stipulation — Undertaking, character of depending on nature of breach — Carriage by sea — Undertaking of seaworthiness.

Contract — Frustration — Charterparty — Time charter — Delay — Time necessary to make vessel seaworthy.

Ships' Names — Hongkong Fir. — Subject matter

By a time charterparty, dated December 26, 1956, shipowners let and charterers hired the m.v. *Hongkong Fir*, built in 1931, for a period of 24 calendar months "... she being in every way fitted for ordinary cargo service ...". Clause 3 of the charterparty provided that the owners should "... maintain her in a thoroughly efficient state in hull and machinery during service ...". The vessel was delivered to the charterers on February 13, 1957, and on that day sailed in ballast from Liverpool to Newport News, Virginia, to pick up a cargo of coal and carry it to Osaka. The vessel's machinery was in reasonably good condition at Liverpool but by reason of its age needed to be maintained by an experienced, competent, careful and adequate engine room staff. When she sailed the chief engineer was inefficient and addicted to drink, and the engine room complement insufficient, and, chiefly for that reason, there were many serious breakdowns in the machinery. On the voyage from Liverpool to Osaka she was at sea eight and a half weeks, off hire for about five weeks and had about £21,400 spent on her for repairs... — Headnote

Figure 3.2 Example of a law report

27

[1962] 2 QB

HONGKONG FIR SHIPPING CO. LTD. v. KAWASAKI KISEN KAISHA LTD.

...

ACTION.

In December, 1956, the plaintiff shipowners, the Hongkong Fir Shipping Co. Ltd., a company registered in Hongkong, bought the m.v. Antrim, 5,395 tons gross, built in 1931, for £397,500 from the Avon Shipping Company Ltd., a subsidiary of the New Zealand Shipping Company Ltd. In the contract of sale the vessel was described as "classed at Lloyds 100 A1. Special Survey passed July, 1955," and the contract provided that the vessel was to be delivered with its class maintained and that she should be taken with all faults and errors of description, but subject otherwise to the provisions of the contract. By a Baltime 1939 "uniform" time charter, dated December 26, 1956, the plaintiffs chartered the vessel to the defendants, Kawasaki Kisen Kaisha Ltd., a company registered in Japan. That charter, so far as material, provided: "It is this day mutually agreed between Hongkong Fir Shipping Co. Ltd., Hongkong, owners of the Vessel called 'Antrim' to be renamed 'Hongkong Fir' ... classed Lloyds 100 A1 and fully loaded capable of steaming about 12½ knots in good weather and smooth water ... and Messrs. Kawasaki Kisen Kaisha Ltd., Kobe, Japan ...

...

| Details of the action

Stephen Chapman Q.C., Michael Kerr and *C. S. Staughton* for the shipowners.

Ashton Roskill Q.C., B. S. Eckersley and *B. Davenport* for the charterers. | Counsel

The following were among the cases cited in argument: Standard Oil Co. of New York v. Clan Line Steamers Ltd.[1] ; Moore v. Lunn[2]; Rio Tinto Co. Ltd. v. Seed Shipping Co. [3] ; Port Line Ltd. v. Ben Line Steamers Ltd. [4] ; Davis Contractors Ltd. v. Fareham Urban District Council [5] ; Tynedale Steam Shipping Co. Ltd. v. Anglo-Soviet Shipping Co. Ltd. [6] ; F. A. Tamplin S.S. Co. Ltd. v. Anglo-Mexican Petroleum Products Co. Ltd. [7] ; Admiral Shipping Co. Ltd. v. Weidner Hopkins & Co. [8] ; Bank Line Ltd. v. Capel (Arthur) & Co. [9] ; Blane Steamships Ltd. v. Minister of Transport [10] ; Inverkip Steamship Co. Ltd. v. Bunge & Co. [11] ; The Europa [12] ; ... | List of cases

Cur. adv. vult.

SALMON J. read the following judgment which, after stating the facts set out above, continued: It has been argued on behalf of the charterers that two letters written on the owners' behalf on September 9 and 10 respectively waived their former acceptance of the charterers' alleged wrongful repudiation. On the other hand, it has been argued on behalf of the owners that once repudiation is accepted the contract is dead, and there can be no question of waiver. It is argued that the letters relied on by the charterers as a waiver could at the most amount to a fresh offer to enter into a new contract on the same terms as the old. Without expressing any concluded view, I am inclined to think that the owners are right on this point. It does not, however, seem to be material since the charterers wrote on September 11 again repudiating the charter, and the owners formally accepted this repudiation on September 13. The position on June 6 was not materially different from that on September 11... | Judgment

Figure 3.2 continued

This less than satisfactory situation led to the establishment of the Incorporated Council of Law Reporting (ICLR) in 1865, who began publishing the official *Law Reports* series. They are the most authoritative series of law reports and are still the preferred series to cite in court. By this we mean, if a barrister uses an authority in court, he or she must use it from the *Law Reports* series in preference to others.[1]

The ICLR state their ethos as the following:

> The cornerstone of ICLR's approach to reporting the decisions of the courts is that only the cases that make new law or change existing law merit reporting in a law report.

They explain their reasoning further:

> . . . cases decided purely on their facts, or through the application of principles that are to be found in cases that have already been reported, have little or no value as authority.

You might well be thinking, 'I've not heard of these 'official' Law Reports? Surely they are not that important?' This is because you generally refer to them by their division:

- *Appeal Cases* – cited as AC
- *Queen's Bench* – cited as QB (when we had a King reigning it was King's Bench, cited as KB)
- *Chancery Division* – cited as Ch
- *Family Division* – cited as Fam

Of course the ICLR are not the only publisher of law reports. In terms of authority, the next best options after the official law reports are the *Weekly Law Reports* (cited as WLR), also published by the ICLR, and the *All England Law Reports* (cited as All ER), published by Lexis.

For criminal cases the *Criminal Appeal Reports* (cited as Cr App R) hold the most authority.

---

1   See also 7.9.8 'Forget about the trees'.

Some series of reports are general in nature (e.g. WLR and All ER), reporting cases from all areas of law. Others are very specialist, only including cases from a particular area of practice. Such reports include the *European Human Rights Reports* (cited as EHRR), the *Lloyds Law Reports* (cited as Lloyds Rep.) and the *Environmental Law Reports* (Env LR), among many others.

Law reports can also be found in newspapers – *The Times* being the most respected of these. Reports in newspapers are released quickly but remember will only be very brief.

3.7.2 Hierarchy of law reports

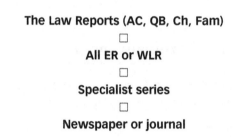

The Law Reports (AC, QB, Ch, Fam)
☐
All ER or WLR
☐
Specialist series
☐
Newspaper or journal

3.7.3 Print v online

These days libraries have to make tough financial decisions and often if a resource is available online they may take the decision to cut the print (saving space, and potentially money). This means that you may find your library does not have a huge print collection of law reports, or it may only cover limited years. It is likely however to have vast collections online via its legal database subscriptions. LexisLibrary and Westlaw hold extensive numbers of law report series; there will be overlap in reports covered but also reports that appear on one service but not on the other. What you find where depends on who owns the rights to the content. Currently the ICLR official Law Reports can be found on both, but the WLR are only on Westlaw and the All ER only on LexisLibrary.

The more specialised series are more likely to be included on just one of the databases with you only being able to view a summary of the case on the other. A fantastic feature on the databases is that often you can access a PDF of the case, seeing it *exactly* as it would be in the print copy. This makes it much easier to read because of their formatting and structure.

Outside the databases, there is a good deal of case law available freely online now. Courts and tribunals will often release case law online within 24 hours of judgment being handed down – the UK Supreme Court judgments have always been available online and the House of Lords were from the end of 1996. Of course now (5 May 2015), the Supreme Court is going further still by creating a 'video on demand' service of past hearings.

Note also that there is one key place to go for case law outside the databases: *BAILII* (the British and Irish Legal Information Institute). Here you will find both case law and legislation, with cases online very quickly after the judgment is given. It does not have the slickness of Lexis or Westlaw but it is an amazing site when you consider that prior to its creation, we had very limited access to case law in the UK, outside of services you had to pay for.

THINKING POINT

Consider the matter of access to justice. Is it appropriate for citizens of a country not to have access to its primary legal sources?

3.7.4 The doctrine of judicial precedent

You will start to hear the term precedent used a lot. Note two things very early on about this term; first note its spelling, it is not president but rather precedent and second it refers to a case that has authority and comes from a senior court and therefore carries a lot of weight.

The doctrine of precedent explains how decisions made relate to each other. It is based on the premise that we all repeat things that we have done successfully in the past so if a case has decided a particular point of law, then it makes sense that future cases on the same or a similar issue are decided in a similar way or at least to look at the previous decision for guidance on how the issue should be determined. That is not to say that change cannot be brought about but there needs to be good reason to depart from a valued decision. Judges therefore, look at decisions from the past to decide what should be done now.

Think about a study technique you have used that has proved to be successful, such as using spider diagrams. You have probably replicated this in other scenarios. Why have you done that? It is most likely because if a strategy works then it makes sense to continue to use it. That is the premise on which the doctrine of precedent is based. If time has been spent in producing a reasoned judgment, which has worked through a number of issues, it makes sense therefore, when something of a similar nature arises, to take guidance from the previous decision to determine the current one.

This is not to say that the doctrine of precedent does not have its drawbacks. For instance, you will rarely find a decision in which the judges clearly state that 'X' is the *ratio* of the case. You have the sometimes rather complicated task, of extracting what the *ratio* in a given case is. This is both a blessing and curse at the same time. It is a blessing in that you can interpret the *ratio* to be something favourable for your argument but it will of course be open to interpretation so that someone else may interpret it differently and you therefore have the task of persuading your listener that your interpretation is the better one. Conversely, once a precedent is set it is then difficult to bring about change because once an agreed interpretation is out there you will have a difficult time to bring about change in that area of the law. Departing from a set precedent is a slow and complicated process.

The operation of the doctrine requires you to have refined your legal research skills so that you are able to sift through the many cases that have been decided in the past in order to find a set of cases that relate to the issue that you are examining (see 4.6.1 for more advice on legal research).

3.7.5 The operation of the doctrine of judicial precedent: *ratio* and *obiter*

Once you have identified the relevant set of cases that you think apply to the scenario that you are dealing with, you need to think about what parts of the cases are relevant to the scenario that you are examining. You will however, be constrained in this task by the doctrine of binding precedent. What the doctrine does is to bind lower courts by requiring them to apply the reasoning of a similar decision delivered by a more senior court. This is to say that courts lower in the hierarchy *must* follow the decisions handed down by more senior courts.

The binding element of the decision is known in Latin as the *ratio decidendi*, which means the reason for the decision. Judges will rarely state what the precise *ratio* is in a given case, which can be difficult but it can equally be advantageous since it offers some scope for determining what the *ratio* of a case is in a way that is

Table 3.1 Operation of the doctrine of precedent in the UK

Court	Application of the doctrine of precedent
Supreme Court	• It binds all lower courts • It is bound by its own decisions – this lacks flexibility; although, since it is the highest court of the land, there needs to be certainty in the law • Exceptionally, it may depart from its own decisions pursuant to the Practice Statement of 1966 where it is felt it is necessary to do justice – this allows the Supreme Court freedom to develop the law according to the current expectations of society • It is bound by the Supreme Court
Court of Appeal	• **Civil Division** – It is bound by its own decisions but there exist three exceptions as set out in *Young v Bristol Aeroplane Co Ltd*:* (i) Where its own previous decisions conflict it can choose which one of the conflicting decisions to follow; (ii) Where its decision which, though not expressly overruled, cannot, in its opinion, stand with a decision of the Supreme Court; and (iii) It is not bound to follow a decision of its own if it is satisfied that the decision was given *per incuriam*, e.g., where a statute or case that would have affected the decision was not brought to the attention of the earlier court • **Criminal division** – It is bound by its own decisions subject to the same three exceptions set out in *Young v Bristol Aeroplane Co Ltd* • It affords itself a wider discretion to depart from its earlier decisions to reflect the fact that criminal law cases can impact on a person's liberty
Divisional Courts	• The different divisions of the High Court are bound by their own decisions subject to the same exceptions as the Court of Appeal
High Court	• It is not bound by the Divisional Courts • It binds all lower courts • It does not bind itself
Lower Courts; Crown, County and magistrates'	• They are all bound by higher courts • They do not bind any courts • They are not bound by their own decisions

* 1 [1944] KB 718

favourable for your arguments. Being able to identify the *ratio* of a case will be a skill that you will develop over some time and in the early days you will find the use of secondary sources helpful in this endeavour. We often advise students that the *ratio* is something that you should be able to plug out of one case and insert into the case that you are dealing with.

What of the rest of the judgment? It should not be assumed that the rest of the judgment does not carry any weight. In fact there will be aspects of a judgment that are influential and persuasive but do not form part of the reason for the decision and therefore are not binding. These parts of the case are known as the *obiter dicta*, which means things said by the way or in passing. The *obiter* should not be read lightly either, because though they are not binding, they can be highly persuasive and over a period of time they can sometimes take over the influence the *ratio* has. In a similar vein, a dissenting judgment can contain very valuable persuasive arguments and you should think about whether it contains any aspects that are particularly useful in how the law should develop in the future.

3.7.6 Hierarchy of the courts

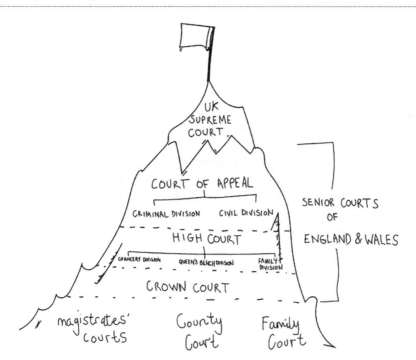

Figure 3.3 Hierarchy of the courts

Table 3.2 Operation of the doctrine of precedent and the Court of Justice of the European Union and the European Court of Human Rights

Court	Application of the doctrine of precedent
Court of Justice of the European Union	• Provides clarity on how European Union legislation should be interpreted pursuant to Article 267 of the Treaty on the Functioning of the European Union – the interpretation of the law must be followed by domestic courts
European Court of Human Rights	• Its decisions must be taken into account by domestic courts but they do not create precedents for domestic courts • UK courts' judgments must be compatible with the European Convention on Human Rights pursuant to s 6 of the Human Rights Act 1998

3.7.7 What can happen to a precedent?

Given that the expectations of society can change over time and information can emerge that can impact the thinking on a particular issue, it must be possible therefore to find a way to amend existing precedents.

There are three ways of doing this, each of which has a different effect:

(i)   *A decision can be overruled*: this means that a court higher in the hierarchy overturns the decision of a lower court in a *different* case and thus deprives that case of its legal importance.
(ii) *A decision can be reversed*: this means that a court higher in the hierarchy overturns all or part of a decision of a lower court in the *same* case.
(iii) *A decision can be distinguished*: this approach is taken by a court when it determines that a precedent that may seem to apply should be avoided because its facts or point of law are different to the case at hand.

3.7.8 Top tips on how to read a case

GUIDE TO READING CASES

(i) What is the name of the case and when was it heard? What does the case name suggest i.e. is it a civil or criminal law case? Note whether it is an appeal case.

(ii) In what court was the case heard and where does it place the decision in the hierarchy?

(iii) What are the pertinent facts and legal issues raised by the case?

(iv) What legal authorities are binding on the court, if any?

(v) What arguments have been advanced by the claimant, prosecution or appellant?

(vi) What arguments have been advanced by the defendant or respondent?

(vii) What is the judgment of the case? Is there a dissenting judgment?

(viii) What is the *ratio decidendi*? If there is a dissenting judgment, what is the *ratio* according to that judgment?

(ix) Are there any important *obita dicta*? If there is a dissenting judgment, what important *obiter dicta* are there according to that judgment?

(x) Do you find the judgment convincing? Why? If there is a dissenting judgment, how important is it?

(xi) Is the decision consistent with other decisions in this area of law?

(xii) Why is this case important and what are the implications?

3.8 JOURNALS: SECONDARY SOURCE

Aside from books, journals are probably the source you will use most within your legal studies. They contain articles on a discrete subject – in a very academic well-established journal this can be 30 pages or so of critique on just one development in the law, or a few cases. It offers a great way to get insight into a difficult subject while preparing for a tutorial, writing an essay or researching for a moot. Unlike books, which are published every couple of years; journals come out several times a year so can be a little more up to date. Other inclusions within journals are book reviews and case comments.

Some words of warning. Some journals can be *very* academic – by this we mean you might find the style of writing a little dense to begin with. Articles will be long, arguments complex and footnotes to other sources numerous. Try hard not to be daunted by this, it is just a case of tuning in and it will become easier with practice. On the flipside, be cool and do not be too wowed by how certain quotations just sound so intellectual that you must crowbar them into your essay. Make sure you understand them fully and that they will add something of value to the critique within your own piece of work. It is often good to try and paraphrase instead in order to force yourself to get the meaning right (more on this in Chapter 6 'Referencing and plagiarism'). If used in the wrong way, this will cast doubt upon the validity of your work.

Authority is very important when selecting a journal; you need to be confident you are letting the views of someone worthy influence your opinion. We don't mean by this that you can only use articles written by professors or QCs, but with the rise of online-only journals and self-published work you have to be sure it can be trusted. Journals come in all shapes and sizes – of the academic type: some are general in nature, covering all subjects and others very specialist, focusing in on one area of the law. There are also journals aimed at practitioners – the solicitors and barristers out there working (rather than researching and teaching the law). Table 3.3 shows a few examples of titles you may recognise in these three categories.

If you are a heavy user of Westlaw you will find a wealth of journals listed there to browse. Many of these are practitioner in nature and would probably be better described as niche newsletters – beware of relying on these too heavily in any

Table 3.3 Types of journal

General	Specialist	Practitioner
Modern Law Review	Lloyds Maritime & Commercial Law Quarterly	New Law Journal
Cambridge Law Journal	Family Law	Law Society Gazette
Law Quarterly Review	Conveyancer	Counsel
Legal Studies	Criminal Law Review	Solicitors' Journal
Oxford Journal of Legal Studies	Public Law	

academic work. The big giveaway is that most pieces would be only one or two pages long; this would never count as an academic article. Note that many of the journals we have listed in the specialist column would actually be used equally by both academic and practitioner readers.

3.9 BOOKS: SECONDARY SOURCE

This will probably be the first way you encounter law at university – students rely very heavily upon their trusty textbooks, and you will find that your lecturer in each of your modules will recommend specific titles for you to use within the course of your studies. Textbooks are not the only type of book you will be using however, and we include a lot more detail on this in the chapter on legal research (see Chapter 4).

3.10 ENCYCLOPEDIAS: SECONDARY SOURCE

A valuable (and often under-used) tool is the legal encyclopedia. You may find some of these on the shelves in your library but you will also find them within legal databases. *Halsbury's Laws* is the absolute king of encyclopedias – it has been published for over a century and if you see it in hard copy you will probably be in awe at just how many volumes there are. It's a great starting point for finding out the law on any given subject – you will be given the relevant primary and secondary legislation, key cases and any related EU law. *Halsbury's Laws* is accessible online via the *LexisLibrary* database.

CATCHING UP WITH OUR FRIENDS . . .

Sienna uses her library training on how to search on the Westlaw database and looks up the decision of *L'Estrange v Graucob* and reads it in full. She feels  satisfied that she has understood the general principle enunciated in the case and that she only developed this understanding through reading the case in full.

Maisy has not yet studied the law on mistake and rectification so decides it is easier for now to pick up her contract law textbook and read the chapter on mistake before she refers to the primary sources of law.

Brodie feels that reading the decision in *Davis Contractors v Fareham UDC* will take him too long and stall him in his research so he decides to read a short excerpt he found through a Google search.

What would you have done differently?

Chapter 4
Legal research: digging deeper

4.1 INTRODUCTION

Despite its desperately unsexy image, learning to carry out research well is one of those skills that will continue to reap you rewards right through your professional working life. As a student, being able to find good quality, relevant materials will prove indispensable for your tutorial preparation, your assessments, mooting and even interviews. As a lawyer in practice, finding sources to back up the substance of your argument is key. For the trainee or pupil barrister, research tasks will be set regularly and this is an ideal way to impress. However for many, this is the skill they struggle with, and frantically grappling with unfamiliar practitioner texts while finding thousands of hits in Lexis can be an isolating and lonely place to be.

While this chapter's aim is to ensure you feel more confident using the sources that should form your armoury, it's worth pointing out early on that you don't need to feel worried or daunted by all this. Law librarians can be found in most law school libraries and, if you're studying in London, also in the libraries of the Inns of Court and the Institute of Advanced Legal Studies. Librarians are blessed with expertise in carrying out legal research (obviously!) twinned with a desire to help others. Note, however, that this isn't about them doing your research for you, but guiding you to the right source for the job and showing you the techniques that make finding something useful more likely. Remember, many will have a law degree as well as years of experience in law firm and academic libraries.

One of the things people find frustrating about research of any type is that there isn't always a 'perfect answer' out there to find. Those moments where fireworks explode in your head and you have to resist air punching while shouting, *'Get in!'* in the silent space of your law library, are not as common as you might hope. As a student, those frustrating moot problems or assessed problem questions are written specifically to make research tricky – clear-cut answers will elude you . . . this is the point! What is fantastic, however, is that the tools you have at your disposal make the research process far less painful than it was for those digitally starved law students of even 15 years ago.

4.2 WHAT WILL YOU BE LOOKING FOR?

As a law student, the majority of the time you spend researching will be spent looking for cases. However you will also want to track down legislation (statutes, statutory instruments and European regulations and directives) and commentary (opinions and reflections) via journal articles and books.

You will also be interested in official reports that might emerge from various government departments or from Parliament. There will be certain organisations that will be of use, for example the Law Commission, who deal with reform of the law in the UK. They produce consultation papers and reports, which will be key to understanding how a law developed and the public feeling around this. It's worth remembering that even just the humble book can come in a variety of forms – each useful for a different purpose:

- *Textbooks* – the books you use to gain a comprehensive understanding of the law in a particular area. These are usually quite hefty volumes and your lecturers will offer some recommendations.
- *Cases and materials* – these books contain relevant excerpts of relevant cases, legislation and journal articles.
- *Statute books* – compilations of relevant statutes in different areas of law.

- *Monographs* – shorter books that go further than just stating the law. Ideal for those who want an understanding around the complexities and debate of a very specific area of the subject.
- *Practitioner text* – as the name suggests, these are used by those in practice. They are very thick, expensive leather-bound volumes on a specific area of the law, and act as 'the Bible' for practitioners in that area. Examples include *Chitty on Contract*, *Clerk & Lindsell on Torts*, *Archbold* for crime. Good for finding succinct detail and signposting to key authorities.

Remember, when reading a book, the unassuming footnotes are worth reading carefully – they will offer other great leads to sources that might shed more light.

THE EVERLASTING BOOK?

You will sometimes come across books where there is someone's name in the title but the author is completely different. Often in law, books go through multiple editions – the original text may have been written 60 years ago and it might be on the fifteenth edition. What changes is that often the original author's name will become part of the title and the writer who takes on the updating will be the author.

You will probably come across *Smith and Hogan's Criminal Law* – the current author is David Ormerod, but the original author back in 1965 was J.C. Smith, who was joined by Brian Hogan for the second edition.

Each piece of work you submit as a student will be marked on the basis of a number of assessment criteria – research will always form part of this. Your lecturer needs to see that you have used sources of quality to back up your own work. Every proposition you make needs an authority to lend it weight. The sources you select will tell your lecturer a great deal about the work you have done.

4.3 BOOKS ON THE SHELF OR ONLINE?

Legal research is no longer something that happens solely when holed up inside a library, flicking through dusty volumes. However, neither is it something you can do exclusively on your trusty laptop; not everything is online yet. You need to have an understanding of both routes and to know when each is appropriate, something that only comes with practice.

TOP TIP

As soon as you start at law school make it a priority to have a wander round the library – work out where all the materials are for your first year subjects, and practice using the library catalogue. It is far better to do this when you don't have the added pressure of an assessment to do. Talk to your librarian!

How a resource is made available (hard copy or online) will be dependent on your university library's collection management policies and budgets. Some titles may be available on the shelf at one university but online at another, for the really lucky students you'll have the choice of both formats. Everyone has a preference and although many like to look at cases online, there are those who feel they can only really take in a judgment if they are looking at the printed source. E-books still have a way to go before they become as desirable as those on the shelf.

You may be surprised to learn just how expensive legal resources are – a practitioner text can be anything from £450–£700, with the online version no cheaper. Legal databases cost many thousands of pounds annually. Libraries clearly wouldn't pay this unless it was completely necessary, which should indicate how essential it is that you exploit these resources as much as possible. Legal information is very expensive indeed and recent years have seen many changes. You will always have to go beyond your favourite online source because different publishers own different content, so you need to be open to this. Smaller publishers who used to allow their content to be displayed on Lexis or Westlaw withdrew it as soon as they could develop their own platforms. This makes it trickier for consumers – the law students, academics and practitioners – as they need to learn the tricks and tips of each individual resource.

4.4 USING GOOGLE AND FREE RESOURCES

'Research' at college or sixth form doesn't really happen – most of the material students put into coursework will come from in-class materials or be plucked from the web, usually via a cursory search on a search engine like Google. So it can be quite a challenge to curtail reliance on this, or understand why your methods have to change.

Google is great as long as you understand its limitations – we use it all the time to find stuff – looking at the last 24 hours of our search history as we write this shows us looking for inspiration for unusual wedding gifts, an instruction manual for a new camera and recommendations for books about Australia (holiday coming up!). We do search for law-related information too, although it's more typical that we'll know what we want and where we shall find it.

Wikipedia has dug us out of many a hole when it comes to needing a bit of information at our fingertips – let's face it, it's the first port of call for most. However it should just be the *beginning* of a research journey and one that you should treat sceptically. This is a website edited by the community – you may have written some Wikipedia content yourself? Do you feel happy about depending on information that could have been written anytime, by anyone? If you're relying upon a source in your written work, you need to be able to trust it.

There are risks associated with looking for information freely available online but as long as you are always wise to them, then doing your legal research via a combination of subscription databases and the free sources online should work well. So what are the risks?

- *Authority* – if you find something freely online, how do you know if you can trust it? Remember, any idiot can post their pearls of wisdom (believe us, we've done it!), you need to be sure of their credentials, particularly before you merrily add a quote from them in your latest essay.
- *Bias* – as above really . . . anyone can post and you need to be sure of his or her motivation. Sometimes even quite 'official-looking' sites can be as flaky as an almond croissant. Keep a close eye on sites of pressure groups – googling will often take you to pages of statistics or policy documents, make sure these are from an organisation that you know is trustworthy, and not from a random group with an axe to grind.
- *Quality* – if you're looking for commentary (someone's opinion on a judgment or the application of a particular section of an Act for example), then it can be very tempting to tap a few search terms into Google in the hope of finding something that is easy to understand. However, you have to be able to judge whether it is of sufficient quality. Your library will subscribe to legal journals, loads of them, and it is here where you should be finding your commentary. For an article to be published in a journal it needs to go through the peer review process. This means that the first draft of an article will be submitted

to the editor of the journal, who will then put it before the board to review its suitability for inclusion in an issue of that journal. They may accept it, reject it or make recommendations for revisions before looking at it again. Academics and researchers make their reputations on what they have published, so the more prestigious a journal, the tougher it is to get something accepted. So make sure you're finding *quality* commentary online.

It is worth pointing out that there are now a number of excellent legal journals that publish solely online, and not in print. If in doubt look at the peer review process on their website, as well as the names of the Editorial Board, take the time to look up their credentials. Great online-only legal journals include the *European Journal of Current Legal Issues* (http://webjcli.org/).

Commentary can also found via blogs – and there are some incredible ones out there. A great all-round blog for keeping up to date with the human rights issues that permeate the subjects you study, is the *UK Human Rights Blog* from One Crown Office Row (http://ukhumanrightsblog.com/). More examples of excellent legal blogs will follow shortly. Again, it is a matter of common sense to ensure the site's quality.

4.5 KEEPING UP TO DATE: CURRENT AWARENESS

Keeping track of new cases and the development of certain areas of the law, as well as careers-related information can be quite tough . . . there are so many places to look. However it's pretty key. When you start going to interviews you'll need to be on top of all the latest changes in the law and have formed an opinion on them. For essays and exams you can't just rely on what comes in your module handbook and crops up in lectures and tutorials; finding those extra nuggets of information are what gain you decent marks.

There are a number of magazine-style journals that are worth checking out. The *Student Law Review* has a very useful section on recent developments (new cases, etc.), which it organises by subject area. This is only available in print, but your library should have it, but if not, the subscription fees are very low for students. For the legal profession, the *Law Society's Gazette*, *New Law Journal*, *Counsel* or *The Lawyer* are useful publications. There are lots of student magazines that your law school will receive too – *Lawyer2b* and *Young Lawyer* are examples of these.

Online is where you will find the greatest selection however, whether it be websites or blogs or via social media. There are too many resources to add here –

you might like to take a look at those listed on the Directory at lawbore.net. However, a few we would say are essential for any law student are as follows:

Halsbury's Law Exchange – www.halsburyslawexchange.co.uk

Head of Legal – www.headoflegal.com

INFORRM Blog – http://inforrm.wordpress.com

Inner Temple Library Current Awareness – www.innertemplelibrary.com

Jack of Kent – http://jackofkent.com

Lawbore – http://lawbore.net

Legal Cheek – www.legalcheek.com

Pink Tape – www.pinktape.co.uk

Public Law for Everyone – http://publiclawforeveryone.com

RightsInfo – http://rightsinfo.org

UK Constitutional Law Association – http://ukconstitutionallaw.org/blog

UK Human Rights Blog – http://ukhumanrightsblog.com

UKSC Blog – http://ukscblog.com

In terms of social media, Twitter is a must-do. So many lawyers and legal commentators use this to discuss, debate and even have some laughs along the way. We have found it hugely useful from a research point of view, discovering new resources and a wide range of views from which we can start to form our own. If a new judgment has just been handed down, Twitter will, within hours, have tweets with opinions, links to blog posts and related cases, the full text of the case and probably a difference of opinion being thrashed out too. There will often be a hashtag generated so that you can search effectively. It is a great learning tool. You do need to put the time in to find out who is worth 'following' of course.

4.6 LEGAL DATABASES

Legal databases are subscription-only websites that contain millions of legal resources, searchable by the user. There are many different databases out there, some deal with all areas of law, others focus on a specific niche. The beauty of these is that you can browse and search in many different ways, so even if you only know limited information you can still locate relevant material. The two giants in this sphere are *LexisLibrary* and *Westlaw* – your law school may well have a subscription to just one or both. Here is a rundown of some of the services you may come across:

- *LexisLibrary* – the granddaddy of legal databases. Users of this service back in the 1990s had to use a massive telephone directory full of codes and type them into a command-line interface to retrieve information – today it is much more straightforward! Find cases, legislation, journal articles, practitioner texts and current awareness here. The focus is on legal materials from England and Wales, as well as the European Union but there is also material available from other jurisdictions, including the United States. A useful inclusion is the legal encyclopedia *Halsbury's Laws* – often a great place to start research.

- *Westlaw* – similar to LexisLibrary in its content, Westlaw contains cases, legislation, journal articles and practitioner texts. Its strength is in an easy-to-use interface and comprehensive journals directory. The Case Analysis tool is brilliant for finding out all the background information to a case: which cases and legislation were relied upon, where it's been used in later cases and which journal articles talk about it. Like LexisLibrary, other jurisdictions are covered but they are a bit of a mixed bag. The United States is quite comprehensive but others are more limited.

- *Westlaw Insight* – part of the Westlaw UK package, Insight is their encyclopedia, ideal for finding an overview of a particular area of law, complete with links to key cases and legislation. It's perfect for getting you started with research.

- *HeinOnline* – an American service primarily, HeinOnline is mainly used for its journals. Unlike the other services it has journal runs going right back to the beginning of their run, e.g. Volume 1, issue 1, which is fantastic. The journal articles are scanned in so you can read them in their original format. They have also developed lots of other packages that your library can pick and choose from. These include the English Reports – those very old 'nominate' reports pre-1865 and various historical or international collections. The search mechanism isn't as sophisticated as Lexis and Westlaw however.

- *Oxford Scholarship Online* – this is a brilliant collection of e-books from Oxford University Press. Bear in mind they won't be textbooks, but monographs, so really useful for getting that more complex information needed to help with the critical analysis you need to get into your coursework.

- *Lexis PSL* – this resource is aimed at lawyers in practice but students will also find it helpful. It is structured by practice area (e.g. competition, family, IP & IT . . .) and has useful practice notes as well as primary legal materials and forms.

- *Lawtel* – often described as a current awareness tool. Lawtel is very good for recent case law summaries, especially those tricky-to-find unreported ones. Also contains an articles index and legislation tracker.

- *Justis* – contains case law and legislation from the UK and EU. There is an excellent visual map of the connections between cases. There are lots of add-on packages from other jurisdictions, which your university may subscribe to, depending on their teaching and research focus. They also have a massive collection of unreported cases.
- *Practical Law* – similar to Lexis PSL, aimed firmly at lawyers in practice. It contains practice notes, standard documents and clauses with drafting notes and updates on new developments. There are also direct links to Westlaw and Lawtel.

There are many databases out there , which specialise in certain specific areas of law, rather than trying to be all encompassing. We've picked out a few below, but your university library may well subscribe to others, again depending on the teaching and research areas of your law school. Remember, the content is very specialised so just using the general resources listed above would mean you'd miss out on the detail.

- *i-law* – this service is split into different packages so your library may subscribe to all or just a few of these. It's probably best known for its maritime law resources, but also has packages on insurance and reinsurance, as well as construction.
- *Jordan's Family Law* – unsurprisingly this service has a focus on family law and includes the leading law reports and journals in this area (unavailable elsewhere).
- *Kluwer Arbitration* – Kluwer has a number of different packages, each of them very specialised. The Arbitration service includes access to the leading law reports and journals in this area (unavailable elsewhere).
- *Oxford International Law* – Oxford University Press has a specialty in international law, and has developed a series of great products, which libraries can pick and choose from. These include the reports themselves as well as the *Max Planck Encyclopedia of Public International Law*. Having a number of services means you can search across content. They also have a free blog, which discusses current affairs while linking to their own and external content.
- *Media Lawyer* – specialist service for media law.

There are also a number of free legal databases – the big two being BAILII (bailii.org) and legislation.gov.uk.

BAILII stands for the British and Irish Legal Information Institute and was formed as part of the worldwide movement to 'free up' the legal web. Prior to its launch

(March 2000) there was no single *zero cost* place the citizen could go for the full text of cases and legislation, expensive databases were the only option. It's a very popular resource, receiving millions of hits per year and is well used by the legal community as well as the 'man/woman on the street'.

To access acts and statutory instruments you can use legislation.gov.uk. A large proportion of the acts included on this site are updated but you need to be careful to check this is the case for each Act you access. Some will only be available in their original form – as of the date of Royal Assent.

4.6.1 There are so many! How do I know which one to choose?

This takes practice – your university library may have created guides online to assist with this however. Usually you need to think carefully about what you need – sometimes *format* is important. If you're preparing a moot bundle you need the case in its published form so you will need to use a site that gives you access to the PDF version (LexisLibrary/Westlaw for example). We've mentioned previously that journals are especially tricky – sometimes a journal may be held in different databases according to *coverage* dates. So you might find the beginning of the run, e.g. Volume 1 via HeinOnline but then the more recent years on Westlaw or via a university press website. Often *jurisdiction* will force you into a particular source; it may be an Australian case you need and LexisLibrary is the only database to include this particular series.

Finally, *subject matter* will dictate this choice – if you want a shipping case then you're likely to only be able to find it on a specialist series like i-law. That publisher owns the leading series of reports and journal in that field so searching on LexisLibrary or Westlaw would be frustrating (you would often only find summaries) and incomplete. The same thing goes for family law – Jordan Publishing previously owned the right to this material so held it within their own product. The likelihood of this changing would depend upon whether the company had been acquired by one of the bigger database providers. If in doubt, always ask your law librarian.

4.6.2 Feeling lazy?

Many of these databases will have ways of pushing information out to you, rather than you having to search all the time. Look out for alerts services – at a basic level they may be able to automatically let you know when there is new content, or if an e-book is updated. The bigger databases have more functionality and enable users to set up alerts for certain content, so either all new content in a specific field (e.g. banking law) or including specific keywords.

4.6.3 What type of research might I be doing?

Almost anything! Research is a broad term and can encompass a quick search for a case and some related materials or ploughing through materials for hours.

As a student your research will usually be prompted by one of the following scenarios:

- preparation for a tutorial;
- finding material to use in an essay;
- swotting up pre-interview on current awareness;
- doing broader reading to enhance the notes made in a lecture;
- preparation for a moot.

Doing thorough research reduces the chance of you missing anything and potentially looking a fool. Your success as a student depends on how you can root out the key bits of information and disregard the irrelevant, as well as making sure you are bang up to date.

REMEMBER!

- There's a massive amount of legal information out there (in the library, via legal databases and freely on the web).
- Sometimes you'll find nothing, other times zillions of hits.
- There isn't always a clear-cut answer.

. . . But knowing some basic strategies for your research will help you know when to draw a line.

The great thing about databases is that they make it a lot easier to do research – they will present a list of results (hopefully including the document you were looking for), but also make lots of suggestions about other related material that might be helpful.

In Westlaw, for example, a basic search for a specific case will show you a summary of your case, where it's reported and give you an indication of the case status, e.g. is it still good law? Clicking on the Case Analysis link will open up a wealth of information, so with little effort you can get everything *around* the case too. But why would you need this extra information?

- *Cases cited* – this shows you the key authorities that were used in the case. You need to know why these authorities were important and how they were used within the counsel argument. Helps you understand the area of law a lot more deeply.
- *Cases citing* – this brings you right up to the present day by showing which cases have subsequently used your case as authority. As with cases cited, you'll also see *how* the authorities were used – was it in a positive way (applied, followed) or negative (not followed), or simply neutral (noted). Looking at those where the case has been distinguished will shed further light on development of that area of law.
- *Legislation cited* – you need to know which sections of which Acts were referred to within the case.
- *Journal articles* – this is the best thing ever for tutorial prep and essay writing. The database has indexed any articles that have some discussion or critique around the case in question. So you don't actually have to search for them. Woo hoo! Bear in mind though, that the availability of these in full text might be limited, so you may have to still do some tracking down. You'll also have to make some value judgments about which journals are most authoritative – some will be heavily academic, others more aimed at practice. Page number count is often a good indication of which is which.

4.6.4 Simple v complex searching

Generally your searching will fall into one of two categories:

1 You know exactly what you want (e.g. name of a case, section of an Act, title of a journal article).
2 You have an idea of what you want but nothing concrete to search with (so you'll have to search using keywords).

For category 1 searches, the databases make this pretty easy for you – both Lexis and Westlaw have boxes to fill in on the front screen for this kind of quick-and-dirty searching. Personally I would always select the tab across the top of the screen for the *type* of material before doing anything; otherwise you could end up with thousands of hits on your result screen. It's pretty rare for you to search across cases, legislation and journal articles all in one go – it would be unmanageable.

Choosing the correct tab also means you get the best search boxes for your task. So for case searching you'll find spaces to fill in for party names, citation and keywords, for legislation you'll have boxes for Act/SI title and provision number, among others.

There is often an Advanced Search option too – don't be scared into thinking this is just for ninja researchers, it just means there are way more search boxes. So you can add lots more detail – things like date range, name of judge and court heard are fields available within the Advanced Search option.

Category 2 searching is a lot trickier as there are so many things that can go awry. There are hundreds of thousands of documents in these databases and you're trying to pick out something very specific. You need to choose the right keywords, put them in the right box and potentially combine them with other keywords too. Confused already?

4.6.5 Choosing keywords

Choosing the right search term or keyword can be difficult – there are so many possibilities! Think about an everyday object and how you would search for that in a database – there are so many options for the right keyword.

Think about a footwear brand favoured by students – words that might spring to mind include the following:

> trainers – sneakers – hi-tops – chucks – allstars – plimsolls – footwear

You might also include search terms for the materials they are made from: canvas and rubber. Other useful terms might be: laces, the sport they are associated with – baseball. You need to choose which keyword or few keywords to search with. Choosing too few finds hundreds, too many might narrow down too much and exclude something important.

Searching for law with keywords is no different – the first challenge your brain has is to first pick out the important bits of whatever question/problem you're focused on. The second stage is to formulate these concepts into solid keywords you can put in a legal database.

TRY THIS!
....

Think about some cases you know really well and pretend you don't know the party names. Test yourself by searching only by keywords. This will really help you to gain an understanding of how pivotal to a search the keywords are. Not getting the 'right' ones can mean no results or zillions of useless cases in your results list. Both are equally maddening!

4.6.6 Natural language v connectors

In Google many people will take the *stick-in-a-few-words-and-hope-for-the-best* strategy. They'll see a million hits and then just look through the first few pages. Mostly this will find what you need (or something close enough). In legal research this isn't sufficient.

You really don't want to be in the situation of appearing in a moot, relying on a case, only for the judge to question why you've seemingly ignored a later authority that overruled this earlier in the year. Using an out of date authority in an essay can lose you a lot of marks if a significant amount of your discussion hinges on it. Our 'judge-made' common law means that you must know how the cases connect up – not something you can always do from one source.

Some databases will let you do Google-esque natural language searching but you are far better off learning some basic commands to improve the relevance of your searching, allowing you to combine your keywords for a killer search.

4.6.7 Master the commands

Think of it as learning another language. Like regional dialects they can vary from database to database but the principles are broadly the same. Students who take the time to get these under their belt early on will reap the rewards.

4.6.8 And/or

The two simplest commands for combining keywords are 'and' and 'or'. It is very rare you would search with just one word – it just finds too many documents. Generally speaking you search for a number of words so you need to be able to join them up meaningfully.

They have opposite effects on a search; here are some examples of a case search:

assault and knife – would find any cases where the keywords assault and knife **both** appear

assault or knife – would find cases where **either** assault **or** knife appear

The first search has the effect of narrowing down, finding fewer results as both the words need to be included. The second has a broadening capacity – finding cases where just assault appears, as well as cases where just knife appears. It's ideal for looking for synonyms.

4.6.9 Phrase searching

A command you might use on Google already is the phrase search. This is where you enclose two or more words in " " to keep them together. So a case search for the phrase "secret recipe" would only retrieve cases where the phrase appears, not where the words 'secret' and 'recipe' appear separately. This can make a massive difference in the relevance of documents you retrieve.

4.6.10 Truncation

To truncate basically means to make shorter, cut something off. When searching you can use this when you don't want to restrict yourself to one version of a word but also find others that start in the same way. It's another broadening search. So you may do a search which includes the word 'tax' and it doesn't find as many results as you would like. As you think more deeply you realise that actually you don't just want to find documents with 'tax' but also perhaps the following:

taxed, taxes, taxation . . .

It's a bit unwieldy to start typing all those words in so you can take a short cut by cutting the word down to its stem, the original search term 'tax' and adding an exclamation mark. So your search now reads:

tax!

The ! acts like a net, gathering in any documents with words that start 'tax . . .' regardless of their ending.

Be aware that it may also find irrelevant results including the words 'taxi' and 'taxidermy'; probably not as helpful!

4.6.11 Wild card

This is like the blank tile in a popular word game – you use it for any character and it will find words that have any letter in that spot. It's useful for searching for words that have similar meaning but only have a one or two letter difference or when you're not sure how to spell something (ie or ei?).

wom*n – would find women as well as woman

int**net – would find internet as well as intranet

4.6.12 Proximity

This is the greatest command at your disposal, and one tragically under-used by students. Imagine doing a search for something – let's say you type in "swimming pool" and negligen! – hoping to find a few useful cases where the words negligence, negligent and negligently might appear (look back at the section on truncation if this is new to you – you obviously read it too quickly!), in combination with swimming pool.

This search will find you over 250 cases in something like Westlaw. Yikes! You can of course use some of the existing filtering tools to narrow this down a bit (by court, date, subject area perhaps), but you might find it useful to think about how you combine those keywords.

A case might be 30 pages or so in length – you might find the first instance of the phrase 'swimming pool' on page 3 but a reference to negligence might not appear until page 12. To make your results as relevant as possible you want the keywords to be *close together*. Both Lexis and Westlaw let you do this, simply swap your 'and' for a proximity connector.

In Westlaw this would look like this:

"swimming pool" /p negligen!

In Lexis it's slightly different but the effect is the same (you also don't do phrase searching in Lexis):

swimming pool w/p negligen!

Both of these basically tell the database to look for the phrase 'swimming pool' within the *same paragraph* as some form of the word negligence.

You should find now that the results you find are massively reduced, but those remaining are far more 'on the money'. If you need to reduce further you can be more precise by specifying within *the same sentence* (Westlaw = "swimming pool" /s negligen! Lexis = swimming pool w/s negligen!) or within X number of words (Westlaw = "swimming pool" /5 negligen! Lexis = swimming pool w/5 negligen!).

4.6.13 Let's see this in action!

Brodie and Ashwin have some preparation to do for an upcoming tutorial. They need to find some examples of cases from the England and Wales jurisdiction that pivot around the problems social media have caused the courts. Here's how they tackle it.

BRODIE
----

1   Goes straight to Google and types in 'social media law cases'.
2   The first page shows links to a BBC article about people getting in trouble for contempt of court by commenting on court cases. It is written by their legal correspondent, so there is some reference to individual examples but no case names mentioned.

3   There's a link that looks promising, describing itself as providing information that has implications for law enforcement and social media. Further perusal sees mention of 'federal and state case law' and 'city attorney' so realise it is US-focused. Not much use!

4   He finds a *Guardian* article speaking about a rise in defamation actions due to social media, it doesn't mention many specific cases but does note Twitter comments by Sally Bercow about Lord McAlpine. Brodie vaguely remembers this in the news a little while ago.

5   Yet more US blogs, which mostly discuss US cases, but there is reference in one to an older case which they describe as high profile – referred to as the 'Twitter Joke Trial'. There's a couple of paragraphs on this so Brodie thinks this will suffice for his preparation, he prints out the BBC and *Guardian* articles, as well as the US blog post.

ASHWIN

1   He goes onto a legal database (Westlaw) first as he remembers a few cases that were in the news in recent times around defamation.

2   He does a case search on Westlaw putting 'twitter' into the free text box and 'defamation' into the subject/keyword box. This brings up a select number of cases, including *Lord McAlpine of West Green v Bercow* [2013] EWHC 1342 (QB). He definitely remembers this one but goes into the case to read the judgment and looks at a number of journal articles linked from the Case Analysis to ensure he has understood the key points.

3   He follows up some of the links within Books to practitioner texts that have relevant sections – *Gatley on Libel and Slander* and *Clerk and Lindsell on Torts*, as well as taking a look through the Cases Cited to look for relevant earlier authorities.

4   Ashwin then takes a look at which cases relating to social media have appeared in criminal actions by looking for 'twitter or facebook' in free text and 'criminal law' in subject/keyword. Clicking *Show terms in context* above the results list allows him to see a little more about each case. He sees *Chambers v DPP* [2013] 1 WLR 1833 which sees a tweet sent in jest taken as a threat under the Communications Act 2003 s 127(1)(a). He reads the judgment and skims through related information as before.

5   Ashwin makes notes on each of the cases he comes across ready for his tutorial.

4.6.14 What do you think of the research strategies taken by Brodie and Ashwin?

Brodie took a completely understandable approach – we all feel comfortable with Google and when you know nothing, going to a database can be intimidating. However even if you use Google as a first stab at a problem, you need to then progress into a database for the detail. Remember if you're reading about cases in the mainstream media this isn't the rigor required – you need to know not just what happened in a case but the legal principles and judicial reasoning.

Ashwin's approach would have certainly taken longer, but he would have gone into that tutorial equipped with in-depth knowledge about some key authorities – not just the headlines! He would have read (at least parts of) the case, looked at commentary via the journal articles to get some varied views and consulted the relevant practitioner texts. An additional step might have been to use an encyclopedia like *Halsbury's Laws of England* at the beginning of the research to pinpoint the key legal areas where social media might come into play – we would see that these were around contempt of court and defamation.

4.7 KEEPING A RECORD OF YOUR RESEARCH

Picture the scene: after a long weekend with minimal sleep you have finally got your essay written, you're gearing up to go and celebrate new-found freedom but think you probably better check the footnotes and bibliography first. You discover to your horror that there are a couple of statements you've made with no references.

This is without question *the* most annoying thing in the world for a student. You *have* to acknowledge any work you have used to avoid being accused of plagiarism (see Chapter 6 'Referencing and plagiarism'). This could have far-reaching effects, from failing the module at a minimum, the other extreme being thrown off the course and your hopes of entering the legal profession dashed.

It takes hours to plough back through all your notes, and all the books and journal articles you've read to see if you can track the mystery reference down. This is without considering all those places online you might have browsed. Save yourself this stress and keep notes of your research trail, however brief. This might feel a bit over the top at first but can save hours later, and is well worth it for a big piece of written work.

Any research trail would include the following type of information:

For books you would need to include author, title, publisher, edition, date and which sections (include page numbers) consulted. For complex works you might need to be more detailed, including paragraph numbers or the keywords you looked up in the index.

When using online sources you would need to note which database you used, which part of that resource (e.g. Cases tab on Westlaw) and the keywords selected.

For either of these types of search you would need to include information about how up to date the source is and when you did your search.

EXAMPLE RESEARCH TRAIL

Aim: to find a 2010 appeal mentioned in lecture about two men who got their own back on a member of a knife-wielding gang invading their home.

Database used: Westlaw

Section: Cases tab – Advanced Search option

Search terms: Using the following fields:

    Free text = knife
    Subject/keyword = revenge and self-defence
    Date = between 01/01/2010 and 31/12/2010
    Case – *R v Hussain (Tokeer)* [2010] 2 Cr App R. (S) 60
    Search done on 20 August 2014

4.7.1 Tools to help

There are lots of tools out there to help you keep a record of useful documents you have found in the process of a search, whether they be a case, section of an Act, journal article, blog post or website. Some are freely available on the web, others your university may subscribe to for an annual fee. Freebie-wise try out *Mendeley* and *Zotero*; for more sophisticated options look to see if your university has a subscription to *RefWorks* or *EndNote*.

4.7.2 In practice

As a trainee in a law firm or a pupil barrister you will be set many tasks involving research early on. Many trainees/pupils find this extraordinarily stressful because (a) it's a way in which skills are tested by their supervisors; and (b) the research they've done at degree and LPC/BPTC level is limited in scope and infrequently carried out. Librarians working in the libraries and knowledge centres of law firms have observed how the research capabilities of young lawyers are severely lacking.

When in practice, any research done would need to be recorded in a report, which may be used as a basis for either written or oral advice. Unlike those 2000 word essays you're most likely to be penning at university, a report to a lawyer in practice needs to be clear and focused in its scope. You'll be summarising the central issues for the client and outlining key findings from your research. Some indication of a methodology (how you did it) will be required but this should form a discrete section of the report, rather than muddying the waters of the issues/findings.

So use the time during your academic course to really gain expertise in the tools to help you carry out legal research. Obviously this will be essential for those essays, tutorial preparation and keeping up to date, but it will really help you once in employment.

CATCHING UP WITH OUR FRIENDS . . .

It is Brodie's turn now – he needs to build on the basic work done by Ashwin in Chapter 2 on academic survival skills – spreading his reading out more widely to take in other sources than his textbook. Let's see what he does . . .

Research trail

Westlaw – Insight Tab – Search box: mistake and contract – finds an overview by Daniel Greenberg: *Formation of Contract: mistake*. Brodie notes some useful summaries here, as well as hints of possible useful cases, e.g. *Agip SpA v Navigazione Alta Italia SpA (The Nai Genova and the Nai Superba)* on rectification. Also links into the practitioner text *Chitty on Contracts* held on Westlaw.

Westlaw – Books tab – *Chitty on Contracts* – Section 2: Common mistake, subsection (c)(f) Mistake and Construction, also Section 5: Rectification of Written Agreements.

Following up on some of the footnotes, he finds references to the texts *Treitel on Contract* (edited by Peel) (31st edn, 2011) and Atiyah's *Essays in Contract* (1986). These don't seem to be available online so Brodie makes a note to check these out in the library.

Brodie also tries *LexisLibrary* – Commentary tab – Browse – Common Law Series: The Law of Contract, looking under Construction – Mistakes.

Chapter 5
Legal writing: weaning off 'like' and 'innit'

5.1 INTRODUCTION: WHERE TO BEGIN AND SOME INITIAL ADVICE

Student writes at 12.05 a.m.: 'Hey what time is the lecture? C U Later Thx'

Do you often wonder whether you should write like this when you are emailing your lecturer or indeed whether you should be emailing them at this time? The short answer to this is NO!

Every month we must receive at least 20 emails each that are a little too informal for our liking. They might start 'Hey Miss' or contain smiley faces and sometimes if the student is feeling particularly affectionate, we might even get a few 'xxx' at the end! All of these examples are inappropriate in an email to your lecturer or any member of staff within your institution. In the dawn of the smart phone era, we are now all prone to receiving more emails than we would like. You need to ensure that what you are saying comes across well and cannot be misinterpreted. You may also find yourself wondering why your lecturer has not responded within minutes. There may be a number of reasons as to why this may be but here are what we think are the top three: it is probably way past your lecturer's bedtime; they too have a personal life and may be out having a good time; the email that you have written is unclear and your lecturer just does not know how to respond to it (see p. 9: Communicating with academics).

Which of the following examples best fits your style of writing? Be honest! Which has the most impact and is capable of being answered in one email?

Ashwin, Brodie and Maisy decide to meet for coffee to discuss details of their upcoming moot. The moot clashes with their lecture, so they decide that it would be prudent to find out if there is an alternative lecture that they can attend. They all email their lecturer:

MAISY

Hey Miss, when is your other lecture? C U later.

BRODIE

Herewith, please find enclosed my humble request to attend an alternative lecture next Wednesday morning. I find your teaching to be most intriguing and enlightening but henceforth I would be grateful, if you could honour this request per se. Therefore, I will purport to attend the alternative lecture on Wednesday. I look forward to receiving your acknowledgment to this most humble request.

Sincerely yours

Brodie

ASHWIN

Dear Mrs Dua,

I am in Group A and you teach me tort law on Wednesdays. I have been selected to compete in a moot, which takes place next Wednesday so I will not be able to attend your lecture next week. Can you please advise me when and where your alternative lecture takes place?

Kind regards,
Ashwin

5.1.1 A Goldilocks problem

Think about which email has the most impact and is capable of being clearly understood. (See Table 5.1, pp. 88–89.)

All opportunities for writing, including essays, emails and sometimes even writing text messages, form part of the process of you developing your writing skills. Subconsciously, you should adjust your writing style according to the context in which you are writing. Writing emails is the form of writing to which most of us can relate. It may not surprise you to note that writing emails forms a huge part of working in a professional environment (see Chapter 8 for advice about employability). You will therefore be expected to articulate yourself and write to a good standard in almost any profession. Getting into good habits now will really help you in being able to ask efficiently for the right information and to convey the right information. We are not suggesting you eat a thesaurus for breakfast and write in an unintelligible manner, but remember, you want people to take you seriously and you want to have your voice heard. When undertaking any legal writing, you need to ensure that the reader can understand your ideas but also that the reader can be persuaded and convinced by what you have written. Starting any sentence then, with the words 'Hey' and abbreviating words that are not naturally abbreviated indicate the following about the writer:

- They are lazy as they cannot be bothered to spell.
- They would rather attempt to look cool than be understood and taken seriously.
- They are unable to distinguish between a formal and informal environment.
- They do not think through what they want to say.

Table 5.1 Maisy, Brodie and Ashwin's emails to their lecturer

Maisy	
Hey Miss, when is your other lecture? C U ltr.	This is just too relaxed and informal. This email does not tell us to what lecture or subject Maisy is referring and overall is far too informal. Would you write like this to your manager or boss? Always address the person to whom you are writing by name. You may use their first name if they are known to you or you could, and perhaps should, address them formally by using their title and surname. Remember, emailing is different to texting. Lecturers and teachers spend an inordinate amount of time teaching you to write well, if you then use abbreviations such as C U ltr, this is rather disheartening but also suggests that you do not take your learning seriously. Also always sign off with your name.
Brodie	
Herewith, please find enclosed my humble request to attend an alternative lecture next Wednesday morning. I find your teaching to be most intriguing and enlightening but henceforth I would be grateful, if you could honour this request per se. Therefore, I will purport to attend the alternative lecture on Wednesday. I look forward to receiving your acknowledgment to this most humble request. Sincerely yours, Brodie	By contrast, this email goes too far the other way and is too formal. It is convoluted and detracts from what Brodie is seeking. Again, he does not tell us to what lecture or subject he is referring. What ends up happening is that when one gets a chance to respond to the email, it will have to be asked what subject and lecture he is referring to and wait for his response before finally answering the initial query. This causes someone in Brodie's position delays and he might not get a response in time to attend the alternative lecture. Remember, lecturers will not be able to respond to emails when they are teaching, and there may be many others to deal with that arrived first.

Table 5.1 continued

Ashwin	This appears to be just right. It is the most
Dear Mrs Dua,	well thought out email. It makes clear what subject and lecture are concerned and
I am in Group A and you teach me tort law on Wednesdays. I have been selected to compete in a moot, which takes place next Wednesday so I will not be able to attend your lecture next week. Can you please advise me when and where your alternative lecture takes place?	Ashwin also states what group he is in so he can be told whether there are any clashes in the timetable if he were to attend a different Tort law lecture. He addresses the lecturer appropriately and with the right level of formality. One can answer his email in one go without sending an email requesting clarity or further information.
Kind regards, Ashwin	

Note, however, we are not saying that have to change your writing habits in every medium; updating your Facebook status and texting your friends probably does not call for such precise language. However, we are saying get into good habits and think about why we listen to what certain people have to say with respect. So the first point to take away from this chapter is (1) to think about *who* you are writing to; and (2) *what* you are writing. Is it clear, or do you think that the reader will have to ask for more information from you, before they can actually respond to your original text?

ACTIVITY

Write how you would/should speak. Read out the following, which you might say out loud and ask yourself whether you would be comfortable in writing the same thing, or whether you would change it. After all, what you write and say should be of the same quality.

> You know that case where the lady used the smokeball to get rid of her flu. That case is so old that we can't use it now.

How might you write about this case and discuss whether it is still relevant?

5.2 THE FIRST CHALLENGE: PREPARE AND PLAN

So now you have had a basic lesson in the importance of writing well and getting into the right mindset. Next we focus on the preparation and planning aspect of your writing.

What is the purpose of planning your writing? Do you think it is sensible to just start writing an essay without thinking about it? When you are about to write anything, whether it is a text, email or an essay you think carefully about what you are about to write; this is even more vital when undertaking legal writing. Do not underestimate the importance of planning.

Some people can think through what they want to write without writing a formal plan while others, like us, need to have a written plan that helps to organise ideas and issues. Whichever style suits you, you should never misjudge the importance of undertaking this step when you are about to write. Think back to when you have written an email or a text message that you wrote without giving too much thought to: when you think about it, don't you wish you had spent a little time on planning what you wrote?

How on earth do you actually plan to write an essay though? Fear not, and prepare to be dazzled by what follows. The secret to planning an essay is that you can plan it in any way that *makes sense to you* as long as you follow these tips:

1   Pinpoint the key areas of interest within the essay title.
2   Research the relevant issues (see Chapter 4 for advice on conducting legal research).
3   Logically organise your material and ideas – what order do you think the issues should be set out in?
4   Keep related issues together.
5   Use chronology when presenting facts.

5.2.1 Popular approaches to planning

Here are some popular approaches to planning, be sure to analyse each one to find your style.

(i) **Mind maps or spider diagrams – both are similar**

Who should ideally use this approach → Do you have a lot of thoughts floating around and cannot seem to get them down on paper? Then these are for you! They are a great way of transferring your thoughts from your mind onto paper.

- These are visual aids and look a lot like a drawing of a spider.
- You have a central body in which you note your main idea or topic and then drawn lots legs or branches from that central body to which you add your ideas or thoughts.
- The great thing about these diagrams is that you do not need to note your ideas down in any particular order, you can add a branch as a thought or idea comes to you.
- Once you have noted all of your ideas, you can then start connecting them and putting them together in a coherent order to make sure that they produce a study idea a bit like a spider's web.
- These are effectively a step up from your scribbled down notes on a bit of paper.
- You can often find really useful mind map or spider diagram programmes online if you prefer them to drawing one by hand, although our preference is to draw them by hand because it retains flexibility and freedom in the creative process of thinking about your ideas.
- You can also elevate this basic idea by adding sub-level ideas and numbering them so that they can form your subheadings in your essays or you can use a different colour for a different set of branches to indicate that that group of branches belongs to a particular idea.
- The key to these diagrams is that they are a great way of getting your ideas out of your head and onto paper in a way that makes sense to you.

(ii) **Lists**

Who should ideally use this approach → Students who do not have a problem getting ideas down on paper but would like to think about how their essay will look and organise their ideas.

- Lists often serve as subheadings or main ideas that the writer would like to develop.
- Lists can also start from flow diagrams, which are then developed into paragraphs.
- This technique is an advanced technique as those who use this feel that they are able to think through their ideas and the order of their ideas as they write their list.
- The list often serves as a prompt to allow you to refer back to your ideas so that you do not lose your train of thought.

(iii) **Writing from the off**

Who should ideally use this approach → The super-confident student, who has enough confidence to write their essay while thinking on their feet, and does not think that they will forget their ideas or how to link them up without a written prompt. Note, we have not come across many students who can do this, so it is probably best avoided.

- This is an excellent position to be in if you can do it. Sadly though, most of us need some kind of memory prompt to remind us of our train of thought.
- This is the most advanced style of planning as you plan as you go, which also makes it the most risky. If you go down the wrong path with an idea, you might find it difficult to change your course of direction. When you write something that you do not plan it can be read out of context and/or require further explanation for clarity.
- A major advantage of this style is that you will become accustomed to thinking on your feet fairly quickly.

Let's see what these look like in practice.

Ashwin, Brodie, Maisy and Sienna have the opportunity to submit a piece of coursework for their Tort Law module and they want to seize the opportunity in order to receive valuable feedback on their written work. They have a choice of two questions that they can answer.

5.2.2 Problem question

Alia is reading a text message while she is crossing the road, when she hears a loud screeching noise before being knocked down by a bicycle ridden by Travis. Upon impact, Alia's phone flies out of her hand and hits Charlie in his left eye and Alia falls so badly that she suffers from two broken wrists.

Advise Alia as to the following:

(a) Charlie has always suffered from a rare eye condition in his left eye, which means that he has to avoid any significant impact to this eye. Unfortunately, when the phone hit Charlie in the eye, this led to Charlie becoming totally blind in his left eye.

(b) Alia is seen in hospital by Dr Dragg. Unfortunately, Dr Dragg incorrectly treats the injury to Alia's wrists. Alia suffers from a great deal of pain in her wrists and so goes back to the hospital five days later where she is correctly treated by another doctor. Alia now suffers from pain in her wrists. Had Alia been treated correctly when she was seen by Dr Dragg, there was a 42 per cent chance that she would not have suffered from pain in her wrists.

(c)   Alia is left with depression after the accident and has become increasingly aggressive. One day a customer asks Alia for some assistance in the shop where Alia is working and Alia refuses to help the customer. The customer tells Alia that if she does not like her job, she should have worked harder at school. Alia is so incensed by this that she takes a pair of scissors and stabs the customer. Alia is now serving a jail term for the incident.

(d)   Travis' bicycle is broken beyond repair, and Travis blames Alia entirely for the accident.

OR

5.2.3 Essay question

The rules on the law of causation are too strict and justice demands a more relaxed approach.

Critically analyse this statement.

5.2.4 Example answer plans

(i)   **Mind maps**
Ashwin prefers to use mind maps with sub-levels and colours.

He would like more practice in how to answer problem questions and so decides to plan how to answer the problem question (see Figure 5.1).

Brodie prefers to use a simple mind map to plan his answer to the essay question (see Figure 5.2).

(ii)   **Lists**
Sienna prefers to prepare lists of things that she thinks she has to go through to answer the problem question (see Figure 5.3).

(iii)   **Writing from the off**
Maisy prefers to just think through things in her mind to answer the essay question. Maisy ponders the question and thinks that she can discuss the current case law and what the problems are with the current test to identify where the rules are too strict and should be more relaxed. While this approach might be good for some and more suitable in essay questions, we would caution against this approach when planning your answer to problem questions. Let us explain why.

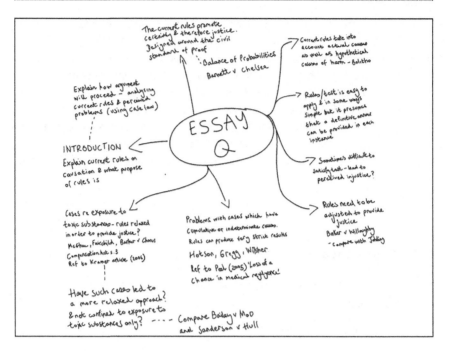

Figure 5.1 Example of a plan for an essay question using a mind map

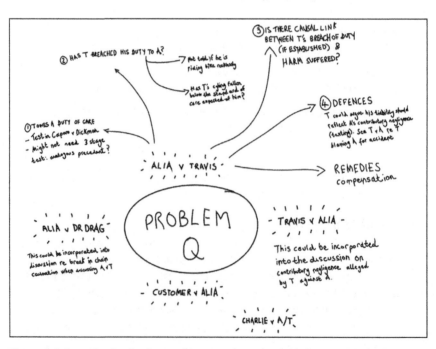

Figure 5.2 Example of a plan for a problem question using a mind map

Who are the parties involved?

A v T
- Alia would most likely pursue a claim against Travis in negligence.
- What harm has Alia suffered? Two broken wrists, possible broken mobile phone and a change in personality.
- Did Travis owe Alia a duty of care (Caparo v Dickman), and if so was it breached (identify the relevant standard of care) and did it cause the harm suffered by Alia (apply the but for test - Chelsea v Barnett)? He was riding a bike but was it reckless?
- Is the harm too remote - maybe not but the change in personalist leading to the stabbing might be see Gray v Thames Trains.
- T could argue the defence of contributory negligence since A was texting and so any damages due should be reduced to reflect A's negligence.
- T could also argue that A's negligence resulted in the damage to his bicycle.
- Remedies - A will be claiming compensation but up until what point? Should she get anything after her criminal act of stabbing the customer.

A v D
- Alia could bring a claim against Dr Drag.
- She could be faced with an argument from T that D broke the chain of causation and therefore he is only liable for her injuries up until that point.
- Query whether the chain is broken since there was a 58 per cent chance that she would have suffered the pain in any event.
- Think about the loss of chance cases such as Hotson and Gregg v Scott.

Customer v A
- The customer would bring a claim of trespass to the person against A
- Unlikely that A could claim for damages after the point of her criminal act since it is a deliberate act.
- Could argue that A would not have stabbed the customer if she did not suffer a change in her personality as a result of the initial accident.

Charlie v A/T
- But for T's negligence, A would not have been hurt and her phone would not have flown out of her hand and hit Charlie in the eye. Although it is A's phone, T caused the accident.
- T must take Charlie as he finds him - Smith v Leech Brain.
- Compensation awarded must reflect that Charlie is totally blind now.

Figure 5.3 Example of a plan for a problem question using lists

There have been many times where we have started to read an answer for which the student evidently had not written a plan (either a mind map or a list) and has clearly gone down the wrong path only to recognise their mistake and realise that they do not now have the time to rectify their mistake, usually because they are writing in exam conditions. It is not uncommon for students of contract law to start answering a question where they have not planned their answer, only to find that a page or so into their answer, the party whom they thought was the offeror must indeed be the offeree. Now at this point, two can things usually happen. The first is that the student can cross out everything they have written and start again, effectively admitting that they have not planned their answer, they got it wrong and now that they have had a chance to think about it, they have changed their minds. Think about how much more efficient it would have been for the student to have spent five minutes planning their answer instead of writing straightaway.

The second option that students often take is to suddenly write in a couple of sentences admitting that who they thought was the offeror must now in fact be the offeree and so they are going to continue their discussion on that basis. Again, it becomes apparent that there was a lack of a plan. Both approaches are inefficient and demonstrate poor planning, not to mention that it reveals to the examiner they are not particularly good at applying the law!

5.3 THE SECOND CHALLENGE: PREPARING TO WRITE

Now that you have your plan set out, you should feel organised and raring to go with your writing. Take a tea break and come back all set to go without any distractions and oh, of course, do not forget to turn your phone to silent!

5.3.1 To whom are you writing?

Always consider who you are writing to; if you are writing to your brother you can, of course be relaxed and informal but if you are writing to the programme director of the LLB or your personal tutor you need to be reasonably formal and professional. Likewise, when writing an essay, remember that the person you are writing to is your lecturer and they will be assessing your written work. They will expect you to put into practice the skills they have been teaching you. Your lecturers use essays in order to assess your level of understanding of a given issue. If you do not write clearly and logically, you are making the task of the lecturer that much more difficult.

You might say that lecturers are paid to understand what you have written and to help you improve your work, which of course is a part of their job, but you do not want to forget that when something is difficult to read or follow it makes it difficult for the reader to understand the argument or the point being made. Your lecturer might then think that actually you are a little confused on the subject and that you have not really developed a good understanding of the issue, however much research you have undertaken. Poor writing skills usually do lead to poor results. Let's then, refer to our top tips for good writing again:

(i)   What are you writing and for whom? Keep it formal.
(ii)   Research the relevant issue (see Chapter 4 on legal research). You would have completed this aspect of your planning before you started to write as you would have used your research to plan your answer.
(iii)   Plan all three sections: introduction, middle and conclusion.
(iv)   Logically organise your material and ideas – in what order do you think the issues should be set out? It makes sense to present issues in a chronological order, since this provides context to the reader and therefore this will help their understanding of what you are trying to convey in writing. By keeping related issues together, your written work undoubtedly has a better structure and helps the reader understand your view on that particular topic better. This approach will also help you to remember to tackle these issues as fully as you can and to make the necessary connections between the issues.
(v)   Introduce each paragraph with a sentence to indicate the topic and make sure that you link and bridge each paragraph so that your answer flows logically.
(vi)   Consider whether the length of your paragraphs and sentences is appropriate. Use a separate paragraph for each new idea.
(vii)   Write in plain English.
(viii) Signpost along the way – the examiner needs to be able to follow your argument so make sure that you do not lose them along the way!
(ix)   Apply your legal research and weave in support from the relevant source of law where appropriate to back up the point that you are making, but make sure that you cite all of the sources that you have used so as to avoid being accused of trying to pass off somebody else's work as your own.
(x)   Directly deal with counterarguments head on and do not be shy about it, as it can often make your argument more persuasive.
(xi)   Always read your work thoroughly before you submit it. Think about whether what you have written is clear – ask yourself whether it would be clearer if you were saying it as opposed to what is written? If so, then write that!

5.3.2 **What are you writing?**

In law school you will typically be asked to write answers to essay questions and problem questions as a method of assessment. While most of you know the difference between the two, it is helpful to remind readers what lecturers are looking for in each.

5.3.2.1 The essay question

In essay questions, lecturers are looking for students' ability to critically evaluate the law. What does 'critically evaluate' actually mean? Take the good lawyer, he or she should not believe or accept everything as it is presented as correct; they should question it and decide for themselves whether they think that the law is as it should be. That is what your lecturer is asking you to do in an essay question. They would like you to consider the current state of the relevant law that is the topic of the essay. That is to say, they do not want you to merely describe it, but rather they want you to consider what is currently good about this aspect of the law and what makes it work well. Once you have considered that, as a good lawyer would always do, you ought to reflect upon what does not work well and why; but do not just leave it there, provide a recommendation on how the law can be improved and what the resulting implications might be.

In order to make these points, you will need to consider your research as well as think about what arguments you would like to make, supporting all of them with primary legal sources (i.e. case law and legislation). An essay question is also ideally where you would want to incorporate your secondary sources on the topic collected through your research. This might include discussions from academic journals on the relevant point. You might have found two or three academic articles on the same legal issue but with three different points of view. An essay question is the right place to present such ideas of others and explain which idea you prefer and why. Imagine if you were having a discussion about an issue. How would you support it to convince the other person that your line of argument is the right one. The principle is the same when you are writing. If you want to persuade the reader of your argument, then you need to support what you are saying. In an essay, you need to support your arguments with specific sources, namely case law, legislation and academic arguments, which may be found in academic articles.

5.3.2.2 Guide to answering essay questions

Remember this guidance applies when you are writing an answer to an essay question in the exam too. Just replace the word research with the word revision – simples!

- **Preliminary steps to undertake before writing:**
  - Consider the question proposed and identify the general area of the law it concerns.
  - Ask yourself, to the best of your knowledge what specific issue does this question concern?
  - Conduct the relevant research following guidance given on research in Chapter 4.

- **The writing stage:**
  - Introduce the legal issue that you think the question would like you to address and set out how you are proposing to tackle the question. For example, you might explain that you think that there are four main areas of discussion and that you will address each one in turn to explain why you think that the legal issue being discussed is ripe for reform.
  - Think about and set out the angle that you would like to take to present your idea. Here are some examples:
    - o Present the advantages and disadvantages of the relevant law and explain what should be changed.
    - o Present a legal argument that you would like to either support or renounce.
    - o Explain why the law in this area is inadequate and should be amended following an example in another jurisdiction.
    - o Compare and contrast the approaches of different judges on the same legal issue.
  - Go through each of the points that you would like to make, ensuring that you start a new paragraph for each point, remembering that it could take you a page to discuss each point. Re-read each paragraph you have written and make sure that each paragraph is presented in a logical manner and as you want it, so that it builds the picture you envisage.
  - Support each point that you would like to make with relevant legal sources.
  - Make a proposal or suggestion with relevant explanations, i.e. the law should be changed or that the example in another jurisdiction should be followed to improve the current status of the law.

- Conclude by summarising your points and making your argument clear, now that you can draw support from the essay that you have written.

- **The finishing stage:**
    - Re-read everything that you have written and make sure that it all makes sense and there are no spelling or grammatical mistakes!
    - Make sure that the order of your arguments sets the right tone to persuade the reader.
    - Check that you have referenced all of the material you have used correctly in your footnotes so as to avoid any accusations of plagiarism or suggestion that you are trying to pass off someone else's work as your own.

5.3.2.3 The problem question

The typical problem question requires you to solve a set of legal issues. This relies on you knowing your stuff and being able to identify the issues presented. The approach is the same with either an essay or a problem question, you need to identify the relevant areas of law that you think the question relates to and then narrow that down to the specific issues that the problem deals with. Now we can almost see you rolling your eyes and thinking, 'If I knew the issues of law that the problem question is getting at, then I would not need anyone's help!'. Think of the situation in a different way. When you do not know how to spell something, what do you do? You use a dictionary to check the spelling of the word regardless using your best guess. It is the same principle with problem questions. You might not know the exact issue that the problem question concerns but you take your best guess and research around that to get to the precise issues involved in the problem question.

Once you have researched the relevant areas of law, consider carefully the instructions. Who are you being asked to advise? Are you advising all of the parties, a few of them, or just one or them?

With problem questions, it is advisable that you always address each issue in the order that it appears. You can, if you find it helpful, use subheadings to signpost to the examiner when you are addressing a different issue. There are two popular ways to do this. The first is to use the names of the characters in the problem question to demonstrate that you are dealing with different claims. So for example this subheading could look like this: *Clifton v Cressida* or *R v White*. Obviously be sure to note the party names the right way around so it is clear who is bringing the claim and who is defending the claim. Another popular technique is to identify the legal issue and use that as your subheading. So, for example, it could be something like this: Is there a valid offer or is there a vitiating factor?

Students often ask whether they need to present 'both sides of the argument' especially if they are only asked to advise one party. The answer to this question is not, sadly, a simple yes or no. It is an answer that will be explained once you have read our most crucial piece of advice. The most effective advice that students have said has helped them through answering a problem question is the following:

> Turn the question into a real-life scenario and imagine that you are a budding lawyer and the person(s) that you are advising is your client and is sitting in front of you asking for your advice. What do you think they want to know and what do they not need to know?

Most clients do not want to know about the history of the law and how it has developed to get us to the current state of the law. You might well need to know this in order to advise the client, but that does not mean that you need to write it down in your answer. The client will rarely, if ever, want you to describe the general area of relevant law in great detail. What they do want however, are answers to the following questions:

- What is the relevant legal situation they are in or relevant issue?
- What is the relevant law that is applicable to their legal situation?
- How does it apply to their situation?
- What is the likely outcome, i.e. is their claim likely to succeed or fail?

Now going back to the question whether you should present one side of the argument or both, especially if you have only been asked to advise one party, think more about the client wanting to know about the prospects of success of their claim. They want to know why their claim might be strong and why it might be weak, as it is only then they can decide whether they should proceed with their claim or what their next legal move should be. A sensible lawyer would advise a client on all aspects of their claim, whether they are good or bad and you should do the same when answering a problem question. That is to say, you most definitely should advise on both sides of the claim so that the party you are advising can evaluate what they should do next.

It is worth noting here that not all cases end up in court. Going to court is an expensive and stressful business. If a case can be settled outside court, the parties may wish to do this, but they can only do this if they have all of the information, good and bad, about their legal situation. Do not be afraid to say then, that a particular party's claim is likely to fail if indeed after your analysis you feel that this is the case. Do not feel that you have to go on to make up a better case for the party if there simply isn't one.

In terms of the writing process itself, you need to support each of your assertions with primary legal sources. Very occasionally there may not be a primary source on the issue that you are trying to support, in which case you should use a good secondary source of law – but be careful to confirm that there really is not a primary source in support of your argument and that you are not forced to use a secondary source due to bad research skills! (See Chapter 4 on legal research.)

Here is an example of how to support your arguments.

Having established that Dr Dragg owes Alia a duty of care, it is further argued that this duty has been breached by Dr Dragg. Dr Dragg's conduct has arguably fallen below the relevant standard of care owed to Alia. The relevant standard of care owed to Alia can be ascertained from the decision in *Bolam v Friern Hospital Management Committee* [1957] 1 WLR 583. This case establishes that a doctor must exercise the ordinary skill of a reasonably competent doctor in their field. This decision further explains that just because a doctor's actions might not accord with another doctor in the field, as long as it is considered as reasonable by at least *one* responsible body of opinion within that field, the conduct will not be deemed to have fallen below the required standard of care. This legal test was further enhanced by the decision in *Bolitho v City & Hackney Health Authority* [1997] 3 WLR 1151 which explains that conduct of a doctor must be able to withstand a logical analysis even if it is supported by another body of opinion within that field. Applying this law to Alia's situation, she continued to suffer a great deal of pain for five days after her treatment and the second doctor who treated her actually treated her correctly and differently, which suggests that Dr Dragg's conduct was not reasonable and therefore fell below the standard of care required of him in treating Alia. Dr Dragg may be able to argue that his treatment of Alia was actually reasonable, but he would need to establish that another responsible doctor would have treated Alia in the same way. On the facts, since the other doctor treated Alia differently, it would suggest that another doctor would not have treated her in the same way as he did and therefore his conduct falls below the relevant standard of care required in this situation.

The next issue to establish is whether Dr Dragg's breach of duty actually caused the harm that Alia suffered . . .

In supporting your argument using a case, you can use another case, which might appear be contrary to your argument. Huh? What did you just read? Yes, remember you want to present both sides of the argument so that you can argue why your take on the argument is the stronger one. Sometimes students think that if they do not show the other weaker side of their argument or if they can hide anything that could make their argument look weak, then they have a better chance of convincing the reader that their argument is a good one.

Actually, your argument will be seen in a far better light if you are able to show all of the weaknesses in your argument and address each weakness head on. Imagine you are a barrister in court, you are presenting your argument in the best possible way and you decide that you do not want to consider the weaknesses of the argument. The barrister for the other side will no doubt raise those arguments in front of the judge and force you to respond to them. Would it not be better if you had got in there first and told the judge that you are aware of the weaknesses and how you propose to deal with them? This method gives very little ammunition to the other side. You should aim to present any weaknesses in your written argument so as to give little opportunity for the reader to pick holes.

5.3.2.4 Guide to answering a problem question

- **Preliminary steps to undertake before writing:**

  - Consider the question proposed and identify the general area of the law it concerns.
  - Ask yourself, to the best of your knowledge what specific issue does this question concern?
  - Conduct the relevant research following guidance on legal research given in Chapter 4.

- **The writing stage:**

  - Separate the legal issues as they appear into separate subheadings if you can.
  - Order each issue in the same order that it appears in the question.
  - Imagine that the party or the parties you are advising are sitting in front of you – what do they need to know and what do they not need to know?
  - For each legal issue identify the relevant applicable law.
  - Apply the relevant law to each legal issue.
  - Advise the relevant party on the likely outcome of their claim – whether it is good or bad!
  - Remember to present the strengths and weaknesses in each argument and to explain which argument you think is stronger and why.

- **The finishing stage:**
  - – Re-read everything that you have written and make sure that it all makes sense and that there are no spelling or grammatical mistakes!
  - – Make sure that the order of your arguments sets the right tone to persuade the reader of your argument.
  - – Check that you have referenced all of the material you have used correctly in your footnotes so as to avoid any accusations of plagiarism or suggestions that you are trying to pass off someone else's work as your own.

5.3.2.5 Answering questions in exams

You will typically be asked to answer either a problem or an essay question in your exams. Use the same approaches above to prepare your answers in exam conditions. Remember, opportunities to write coursework throughout the year provide you with practice of how to answer questions in exam conditions.

5.3.3 Using your plan of action and research to write

Now you have sorted out your style for both essay and problem questions, let's turn our attention to what you need to write about.

The most common format used for law essays is one that has a beginning, middle and end. You need to introduce your ideas and arguments to the reader, developing those ideas and arguments by providing your analysis and reasoning. Finally, you need to round up your ideas and arguments to finish your essay. This is the general expected format whether you are answering an essay question, a problem question or even if you are writing an extended essay.

5.3.4 Legal writing demystified

How many times have you said to someone, 'but that is what I meant' when talking about something that you have written whether it be a text, email or formal piece of work?

Writing clearly is vital. What you actually mean and what you actually write may not be the same thing. This is a common problem. Many a time has a student said to us when discussing the drawbacks of their essay: 'but that *is* what I meant'.

Making sure that the words you use convey what you actually mean is a difficult but essential task.

Now you have the tools to write, you need to think about your writing style itself and actually getting your arguments down on paper.

The secret to legal writing is to write well in general. There is nothing particular about writing in the legal profession that is not true of good writing in general. Many students feel that because they are studying law, they need to write in almost a foreign language to get high marks. That is not the case! Students need to write in plain English so use the English that you already know. It is true to say though, that you will have to use legal terms and you might even incorporate some newly learnt words in English; but you still should only write in the ordinary way without trying to use words that you do not understand!

ACTIVITY

Find your mobile phone contract and read the terms and conditions – OK, yes there are a lot, so just read the fifth and tenth clauses. Do you actually understand what they mean? How else could they be drafted in order to convey the message more clearly?

Reading out what you have written is massively helpful because if it does not sound right, you know that you need to redraft it. If someone is around (you can even do this in front of your dog, cat or a mirror), ask them if they will listen to what you have read. You will soon realise if what you have written needs to be redrafted. This little exercise will not only improve your written skills, but it will also improve your public speaking skills.

The best advice that we can give you and which we give to our students is to read a recent judgment. Give it a try by reading this short extract from in the case of *Montgomery (Appellant) v Lanarkshire Health Board (Respondent) (Scotland)* [2015] UKSC 11:

Introduction

1   Nadine Montgomery gave birth to a baby boy on 1 October 1999 at Bellshill Maternity Hospital, Lanarkshire. As a result of complications

during the delivery, the baby was born with severe disabilities. In these proceedings Mrs Montgomery seeks damages on behalf of her son for the injuries that he sustained. She attributes those injuries to negligence on the part of Dr Dina McLellan, a consultant obstetrician and gynaecologist employed by Lanarkshire Health Board, who was responsible for Mrs Montgomery's care during her pregnancy and labour. She also delivered the baby.

2   Before the Court of Session, two distinct grounds of negligence were advanced on behalf of Mrs Montgomery. The first concerned her antenatal care. It was contended that she ought to have been given advice about the risk of shoulder dystocia (the inability of the baby's shoulders to pass through the pelvis), which would be involved in vaginal birth, and of the alternative possibility of delivery by elective caesarean section. The second branch of the case concerned the management of labour. It was contended that Dr McLellan had negligently failed to perform a caesarean section in response to abnormalities indicated by cardiotocograph ('CTG') traces.

3   The Lord Ordinary, Lord Bannatyne, rejected both grounds of fault: *[2010] CSOH 104*. In relation to the first ground, he based his decision primarily on expert evidence of medical practice, following the approach laid down by the majority in *Sidaway v Board of Governors of the Bethlem Royal Hospital and the Maudsley Hospital [1985] AC 871*. He also concluded that, even if Mrs Montgomery had been given advice about the risk of serious harm to her baby as a consequence of shoulder dystocia, it would have made no difference in any event, since she would not have elected to have her baby delivered by caesarean section. That decision was upheld by the Inner House (Lord Eassie, Lord Hardie and Lord Emslie): *[2013] CSIH 3; 2013 SC 245*.

4   The appeal to this court has focused on the first ground of fault. The court has been invited to depart from the decision of the House of Lords in *Sidaway* and to reconsider the duty of a doctor towards a patient in relation to advice about treatment. The court has also been invited to reverse the findings of the Lord Ordinary in relation to causation, either on the basis that his treatment of the evidence was plainly wrong, or on the basis that, instead of applying a conventional test of 'but for' causation, he should instead have applied the approach adopted in the case of *Chester v Afshar [2004] UKHL 41; [2005] 1 AC 134*.

5   Before considering those issues, we shall explain in greater detail the relevant facts and the approach adopted by the courts below.

Yes, it is written by a learned judge, who has had many years of experience, but look at the language, style and clarity that he has used. There is nothing convoluted in this excerpt and it is very clear and easy to understand. This judgment is not written in a way that is convoluted or difficult for one to understand. It is not verbose nor is it written in a deliberately awkward manner. Each issue is separated into its own paragraph and the sentences are not overly long. So what is stopping you from writing in such a way? You too should always remember that you need to write clearly and concisely.

If you want to start putting some of this into practice before your next essay is set, then maybe start using these tips everyday whether you are writing an email, text message or simply updating your social media status. After a short while, they will become habit and half of the challenge in writing law essays will be overcome!

5.3.5 Editing

Remember, you want your written ideas to come across effectively and to do that, you need only use words that will help you in that endeavour and no more. When you finish writing your essay and are re-reading it, ask yourself the following question: are there any words that you can take out while keeping the same sense and meaning within the sentence? If the answer is yes, then the word is extra and does not help you in putting your idea across effectively. In fact, it probably has the opposite impact.

If removing the word makes the sentence weaker and prevents the reader from understanding your idea, then keep it in. You may find it helpful to use Strunk's *The Elements of Style* on how to improve your style. This may transform your style of writing.[1] Assess what you like and dislike when you read your work and note that good writing makes the reader's job easy; bad writing makes it difficult. You don't want to make the person reading your work sweat too much – remember you are hoping they will reward you with lots of marks!

---

1   William Strunk, Jr and E.B. White, *The Elements of Style* (4th edn, Longman 1999).

5.4 THE THIRD CHALLENGE: UNDERSTANDING THE FEEDBACK

Once you have submitted your essay, you will no doubt be eager to receive feedback on your work. It is helpful to be aware of some of the feedback that lecturers provide on written work so you know what it means and how you should use it to improve your work. Such comments may cover the content of your legal argument as well as notes on your use of language, structure and even grammar. Now you might wonder why it is appropriate for your lecturer to pass comments on the style and language of your work, but this goes back to what was explained earlier: good writing is essential to succeed in good legal writing. There should be no doubt over what you have written and what you mean. Table 5.2 shows some of the main comments that you might come across.

Table 5.2 How to understand feedback and improve your work

Feedback	What it means	How to use it to improve your work comment
Explain, unclear or clarify	What you have written is unclear without any further explanation.	This is an issue relating to style and you need to read through the sentence again. Read it out loud to someone else if you can, otherwise read it aloud in front of the mirror. The chances are that the other person does not understand what you have written. If you have to add a couple of sentences to explain your original sentence to them then that is a problem: the reader cannot understand your idea without further information and clarity. **How to improve**: re-read your work when it is finished, possibly in front of someone else if you can. Ask yourself whether further information is necessary to convey your idea or whether what you have written is enough?
Wordy/ verbose	Extra words have been used to take up space and your argument is lost in a sea of words.	Cramming in extra words prevents your ideas coming across effectively: they will be lost to the reader in all of the additional (and unnecessary) words. **How to improve**: when you are re-reading your essay, ask yourself the following question: are there any words that you can take out while

Table 5.2 continued

Feedback	What it means	How to use it to improve your work comment
Wordy/ verbose *cont'd*		continuing to convey the same idea without it? If the answer is yes, then the word is extra and does not help you in putting your idea across effectively. In fact, it probably has the opposite impact. If losing the word makes the sentence weaker and prevents the reader from understanding your idea, then keep it in.
Good	The point is well made and is understood by the reader. The legal content is also correct.	The section marked good is the style that you should be adopting throughout your essay. **How to improve**: try to identify the style that you have adopted and try to replicate it in your writing as you know it has been successful.
Authority	The marker is asking you what law supports what you have written.	A key rule in legal writing is that you must support your ideas with law. You can use a case (sometimes called an authority), legislation or a secondary source of law. **How to improve**: unless you are presenting an original idea, you need to back up what you have written with law otherwise the reader is not going to be persuaded by it or impressed.
Awkward	Your sentence or idea is presented in an odd way, which could be written better.	The idea that you are trying to make is not being conveyed very clearly and is written in a clumsy way. **How to improve**: a good way of trying to improve what you have written is to say it out loud and write it down as you have said it, you may find that you are able to articulate yourself better just by saying what you want to say out loud.
Padding/ too long	You have written more than needed; and not all of it is relevant.	Examiners are good at spotting when a student is just trying to fill the space. You may only have a small comment to make but feel that it will not gain the right level of consideration from the examiner because it is so short.

Table 5.2 continued

Feedback	What it means	How to use it to improve your work comment
Padding/ too long *cont'd*	You may have added in extra information to fill space to make your argument look more substantial than it is.	Remember, the examiner is looking for your ability to understand, apply and analyse legal concepts. It is important then, that you do not detract from this by cloaking what you are really trying to say in needless words. **How to improve**: re-read your work and ask yourself if everything that you have noted is really relevant, if not then delete it. A few words can be more powerful than many.
Apply the law	You may have demonstrated that you have identified the right area of law applicable and you may even have described it but you have failed to apply it to the facts with which you have been presented.	A fundamental skill that examiners look for is the ability to apply the law to a given set of facts. This is usually tested in problem-based questions. It is not enough for a student to describe the relevant law since even the average person could describe the relevant law by looking it up. The real skill lies in applying the law to a given set of facts. **How to improve**: imagine that you are a qualified lawyer and the client is the character from the problem question and is sitting in front of you asking for advice. What do you think that they would like to know? They would like to know what relevant law applies to their situation, how it actually applies to their situation and what the implications are, i.e. are they likely to have a strong claim?
Relevance	It is unclear to the reader what the relevance of what you have written is to the questions that you are trying to answer.	Have you ever heard the advice 'always refer back to the question?' Well this is relevant here! You always need to demonstrate why and how what you are writing relates to the question set. If it does not relate to the question set, it is most likely to be considered as padding. Sometimes, however, you might have a light-bulb moment and think I must note this point, but what you forget to do is to explain what the significance of the point is.

Table 5.2 continued

Feedback	What it means	How to use it to improve your work comment
Relevance *cont'd*		**How to improve**: as a rule you should always plan your answer in advance of writing it. This provides you with a clear structure and guidance on what you should include in your answer. This is also a way to keep you on track in terms of making points that are relevant to the question set and should prevent you from going off on a tangent. Also make sure that you question your work. Always ask yourself how and why does your argument answer or deal with the question set. Have you fully explained your brilliant idea?
Informal	You have written in an inarticulate manner, which can suggest a lack of attention to your work.	In a world in which we spend a lot of time on social media, it is easy to forget that you need to write formally and not informally innit? Do not forget that training in law, whether you decide to become a lawyer or not, consists of being able to articulate yourself well both verbally and in your written work. You will soon discover that a misplaced comma or a misplaced 'or' in a sentence can change the meaning of that sentence completely. It is therefore imperative that you write clearly and precisely. You want your written work to be taken seriously and for it to convey precisely what you mean. Writing informally gives the impression that you are looking for shortcuts and often cannot be bothered to think about what you are writing. Think about it, what would you trust or be persuaded by more, something written formally or informally? **How to improve**: get into good habits in your everyday writing. So write formally in your text messages or your social media updates and feeds. Slowly but surely, the good habit of writing formally should come naturally to you.
Style/ layout	You should have thought about the presentation or order of your	A key aspect to good legal writing is to be able to present your legal arguments in a logical manner. This is not the same as saying that there is only one correct order in which to present your arguments, but rather that the

Table 5.2 continued

Feedback	What it means	How to use it to improve your work comment
Style/ layout *cont'd*	ideas and arguments a little more since the current presentation does not flow very well.	order that you have used does not seem to be intuitive. While creativity and originality is encouraged, there are aspects of the law that follow a certain pattern or order. So, for example, it does not make sense to consider whether a contract has been breached if you have not first considered whether the contract has been validly formed. In some other cases it may be that you are dealing with issues in an order that does not seem suitable.
		How to improve: if you are answering a problem question, tackle issues in the question in the order in which they appear and apply the relevant law in the way that it is formed. If you are dealing with an essay question, then think about how you want your argument to unfold in that you want to be able to take the reader step by step through your point so that they are persuaded by it. Highlight why each point connects with the other.
Grammar/ syntax/ spelling	The structure of your sentence is not correct or the order of your words does not form a good sentence. You may also not have used appropriate punctuation. You may also have misspelt some words.	As has been said many times in this chapter already, the arrangement, order or articulation of words is critical to good legal writing. It is therefore important that you order your words in each sentence appropriately and use the correct punctuation so that your argument can be interpreted correctly. You would have learnt from our discussion on statutory interpretation how carefully scrutinising words is a skill that budding lawyers need to develop. Equally then, budding lawyers need to write using good grammar and avoid convoluted syntax.
		How to improve: a quick and modern way around this is to run any typed work through a spelling and grammar check function that may be available. This, however, will not help you if the order of your words is not appropriate or if the sentence reads reasonably well but conveys another meaning to a lawyer. Also you may

Table 5.2 continued

Feedback	What it means	How to use it to improve your work comment
Grammar/ syntax/ spelling *cont'd*		misspell words in a way that forms another word that is spelt right but not the word that you wanted to use. For example, you want to write precedent but instead you spell it wrong and write president. Both words are spelt correctly but only one of them is appropriate for your sentence. This can only be fixed with patience, practice and a lot of reading. You need to re-read your work carefully and look at whether the sentence both looks and sounds right. The more you read the better you will become at composing sentences and identifying bad spelling (see Strunk's *The Elements of Style* for further advice on legal writing).
Descrip- tive/lacks analysis	You have merely described what you believe to be the relevant law but you have not applied it to the scenario.	Some students tend to lack confidence when answering a question and think that if they describe everything they know about the relevant area of the law, they will be given credit for it. While it is true that some credit will be given for identification of the relevant area of law, it will be minimal. The marker is familiar with the relevant law and therefore does not need you to recount it but rather to apply it to the facts and/or critically analyse it. Answering questions for your assessments is not a memory test. While you do need to remember and recall the relevant law, generally you will be asked to apply it or analyse it. You only need to set out or explain the relevant law to an extent to alert the marker that you have identified the correct area of the law and having done that in a few sentences, you are now going to apply or analyse it.

How to improve: as with the advice given on 'apply the law', imagine that you are a qualified lawyer and that the client you need to advise is sitting in front of you. The person that you are advising could be anyone: someone who is dealing with a breach of contract; an individual |

Table 5.2 continued

Feedback	What it means	How to use it to improve your work comment
Descrip-tive/lacks analysis *cont'd*		who has suffered from some form of negligence; or even an organisation like the Law Commission. What do you think your client would like to know? Would they like a long description of the law and nothing else, or would they like a short description of the law for context and then examples of its application or an illustration of how it can be improved?
Reference/ citation	You have failed to attribute the source from where the work comes.	Sometimes students will present an idea but fail to tell the reader where it actually comes from. It may therefore appear that the student is trying to pass off that idea or work as their own. That unfortunately can be classified as something called plagiarism (see Chapter 6). Plagiarism is a serious offence, particularly for law students, because it suggests that the student is dishonest. That is a mark no student (or any other person for that matter) should want against their name. Lawyers are deemed to be honest professionals who can be trusted in the community. If you are suspected of plagiarism, your tutor will note this and you will be given an opportunity to explain the situation. If you are found guilty of plagiarism, this will be noted in your student file and may of course be disclosed in all of your future references. As you can imagine, this may scupper your chances of progressing within the law.
		Cases should also be cited with their full citation when they are mentioned for the first time. Not doing so looks lazy and also indicates that you have not undertaken the relevant research. It is also important that you identify, in the citation, the exact paragraph or page number to which you are referring if you are referring to a particular idea in the case or point. If the reader wants to check that point that you are making, they may do so if they have that information.

Table 5.2 continued

Feedback	What it means	How to use it to improve your work comment
Reference/ citation *cont'd*		**How to improve**: always err on the side of caution and add in a footnote attributing the author of the idea or the quote. Get into a good habit of noting down the full reference of everything that you read when you are researching to write. You can use various apps for this (see Chapter 6) and these help you develop good habits. It also stops those 2 a.m. panics just before a deadline when you cannnot remember where a particular idea came from! In terms of cases, make a quick note of the case, but most importantly the page or paragraph number because it is not hard to find the citation of a case but it is harder to find an exact point in case. Failing to do this may mean that you have to read the whole case again, which might be 80 pages long!

CATCHING UP WITH OUR FRIENDS . . .

Ashwin starts to prepare his speech as senior appellant for his upcoming moot. He does not want to use this speech as a script but rather wants to practise setting out his arguments in full and use this opportunity to practise writing more. Ashwin likes to use subheadings in his writing especially where this helps him signpost to the reader what point he is making. Here is an extract of his speech:

. . .

As regards the construction of the contract, the Court of Appeal in *East v Pantiles (Plant Hire) Ltd* explains that it is possible to correct precisely the type of mistake that Linda is looking to have corrected.*

> [A] mistake in a written instrument can, in certain limited circumstances, be corrected as a matter of construction without

obtaining a decree in an action for rectification. Two conditions must be satisfied: first, there must be a clear mistake on the face of the instrument; secondly, it must be clear what correction ought to be made in order to cure the mistake.

Clear mistake

Linda is advised to argue that there is a clear mistake on the face of the instrument, namely a clerical error in the drafting of the clause. Linda made clear to Bulldozer that she would like to host her daughter's birthday party on 11 June and therefore would need a few days to set up her house prior to the party. If the work were to be completed on 10 June this would leave her no time to set up for the party and she would have to find an alternative venue for it. The bonus payment should not therefore be payable to Bulldozer.

What correction ought to be made?

The contract should be corrected to read that the work should be completed on 1 June.

Since both of these conditions are satisfied, then the correction can be made as a matter of construction. This argument is further supported by the decision in *Chartbrook Ltd v Persimmon Homes Ltd* [2009] 1 AC 1101.** This decision explains that the background leading up to an agreement can sometimes be taken into account when trying to determine whether the agreement contains a clear mistake and this is part of the overall exercise of interpreting the contract.

---

* (1981) 263 EG 61, – *East v Pantiles (Plant Hire) Ltd* [1982] 2 EGLR 111, 112.

** [2009] 1 AC 1101, 1114.

Chapter 6
Referencing and plagiarism: borrow don't steal

6.1 INTRODUCTION

Any piece of work you submit will be a mixture of your own words and those of others. Whether it's a problem question, essay question or dissertation, you will need to make clear where those quotes, ideas and analysis came from originally.

When starting out at university you will find it tricky to weave your own 'voice' into the views of others in writing, but it is something that becomes easier with practice.

Each point you make will need to be 'backed up' with reference to a primary or secondary source. You may include a quote from a particular judge or the controversial view of an academic on a particular judgment. Each of these would require a note being made of where you found the original information (you may remember this from Chapter 4 on legal research).

There are several reasons for this; first it is good old-fashioned manners. If you borrow something, whether it be your sister's favourite jacket, your mum's car or your mate's games console, you should really ask politely first. It's unworkable to imagine all the law students in the UK asking permission of law reporters, judges and legal commentators, before submitting essays. The world would grind to a halt. So we have a system where we reference any sources within our essay, giving credit to the original authors.

The second reason is that by not doing so, you are leaving yourself exposed and at risk of being found guilty of something called **plagiarism**, which can have severe consequences.

As with most offences, there is a scale of plagiarism – from those who buy essays off the internet and submit them as their own work (yes, there really are people stupid enough to do this!) to those slapdash sorts who include the odd quote or concept that comes from 'something they've read' but they fail to acknowledge it. In Chapter 5 on legal writing you'll see something useful on this in section 5.4 'Understanding your feedback'.

6.2 SO WHAT EXACTLY IS PLAGIARISM?

Plagiarism is the presentation of someone else's ideas or words as your own, including them within a piece of work without any reference or credit given. This could be something textual – incorporating a quote from an article you've read into your essay without acknowledging the author, but it applies equally to other media too – data, graphs, illustrations, film, podcasts, computer code, even music.

In simple terms, it is pinching something good from someone else and inserting into your own work to make it sound better!

Lethally, it can even be done entirely innocently; you might read something and not make a note of it. Later, when writing the essay, you might include the idea; perhaps thinking it is your own insight. Or despite having a sneaking feeling it wasn't entirely you, you can't find a reference in your notes so you just pop it in and hope no one notices.

You need to develop an understanding of what good academic practice entails. This is your best protection against plagiarism.

6.2.1 Sounds complicated – are there different types?

Not really and yes. (See Table 6.1 below for examples of different types of plagiarism.)

Table 6.1 Types of plagiarism

Verbatim – word for word quotation	This is where you find a quote that just sums up perfectly what you want to say. You put it in your essay, surrounded by your own words, but don't use quotation marks to distinguish the bits that aren't yours, or reference the source.
Copy and paste	Common when researching on the internet, this is an easy trap to fall into. You find something useful, do a nifty ctrl-C and then paste it into your essay. Easy to forget you need to add a footnote, but without acknowledging the source this is plagiarism. Remember from Chapter 4 on legal research that information you find freely on the internet (rather than via published journals) needs to be treated with more caution anyway.
Paraphrasing	You'll probably be familiar with this – you put another person's work into your own words. This can vary in terms of the extent of paraphrasing: from just altering a couple of words and changing the order, to providing a summary of what you've read entirely in your own words. The latter option is far preferable. Remember, even though you are not using someone else's words, you are using their ideas so you must credit them, making it clear within the text and footnote where this comes from.
Collusion	If you work with others you must declare this. Unless it is a group project all work you submit should be your own, and no one else's. Do not try to deceive if this is not the case.
Self-plagiarism	This one is the most surprising: you can plagiarise *yourself*. Quite often students writing dissertations might decide to do this extended piece of work based on some element that interested them in an earlier essay. If they use any excerpt from the previous work then it must be referenced.

6.2.2 Not convinced? Four facts for would-be plagiarists

1   Most universities now ask students to submit work online – it is then run through a tool that automatically checks for percentage of similarity to the work of others, both your peers and that found online.
2   Your lecturers are experienced researchers who often live and breathe their subject – they know all the key articles written in that area. Don't try and pretend those words are yours! The flipside of this is that by avoiding plagiarism and acing your referencing your lecturers will be suitably impressed – they look to footnotes for an indication of the quality of your research.
3   There's no shame in using the words of others – you are demonstrating your skill by the research you've done in finding them and the critical analysis you do in dissecting the sources and bringing them together in an engaging way.
4   Plagiarising can mean failing a module or in extreme cases being thrown off the course altogether. Most training contract applications want to know what you scored in individual modules – don't jeopardise this!

6.2.3 University plagiarism policies

Every university will have their own policy on plagiarism, which will include a breakdown of types of plagiarism (some variation on the information given above) as well as details of the penalties that will follow if you are found to have fallen foul of this policy.

It is sensible to read this policy carefully; you need to have a good understanding of what rules are. Remember penalties can include losing marks, or being hauled in front of an academic misconduct panel – ignorance of plagiarism will not protect you, so make sure you understand.

6.2.4 Plagiarism and the legal profession

The Solicitors Regulation Authority (SRA) sets out its expectations of trainee solicitors and qualified lawyers in their Suitability Test,[1] laying out the ten mandatory principles expected to be adhered to. Here they are:

---

1   SRA, SRA Suitability Test 2011, Version 14 (30 April 2015). www.sra.org.uk/solicitors/handbook/suitabilitytest/content.page, accessed 30 August 2015.

You must:

1   uphold the rule of law and the proper administration of justice;
2   act with integrity;
3   not allow your independence to be compromised;
4   act in the best interests of each client;
5   provide a proper standard of service to your clients;
6   behave in a way that maintains the trust the public places in you and in the provision of legal services;
7   comply with your legal and regulatory obligations and deal with your regulators and ombudsman in an open, timely and co-operative manner;
8   run your business or carry out your role in the business effectively and in accordance with proper governance and sound financial and risk management principles;
9   run your business or carry out your role in the business in a way that encourages equality of opportunity and respect for diversity; and
10   protect client money and assets.

You'll see the reference to this Suitability Test in footnote 1 – go and look at the website; it goes on to note several points relevant here. Section 2 is about disclosure – failing to disclose information relevant to your application (e.g. being disciplined for plagiarism at university) will be seen as evidence of dishonesty. Section 4.1 concerns assessment offences:

> Unless there are exceptional circumstances we will refuse your application if you have committed and/or have been adjudged by an education establishment to have committed a deliberate assessment offence which amounts to plagiarism or cheating to gain an advantage for yourself or others.

This is serious stuff – you might do something silly at university and it will prevent you from entering the profession. A guidance note clarifies 'exceptional circumstances' to infer that their focus will be on any activity classed as 'cheating or dishonesty', so incorrect referencing may not always fall under this. However, do you want to take this risk?

6.2.5 Plagiarism and the real world

Plagiarism isn't just something that happens within the thrilling world of academia, passing someone else's ideas off as your own happens out there in the real world too. Coldplay, Beyoncé and J.K. Rowling have all been accused of it in recent years in relation to their creative output. More recently, the writers of the biggest selling song of 2013, Pharrell Williams and Robin Thicke, were found to have copied Marvin Gaye's 1977 song 'Got to give it up' in their massive hit 'Blurred lines'.[2]

Journalists working at various international newspapers have been 'found out' for lifting quotes, borrowing content and fabricating events. Lawyers are not immune from this temptation either; an Iowa lawyer was found guilty of plagiarising verbatim 17 out of 19 pages of an article for his pre-hearing brief in 2007.[3]

6.2.6 OK, OK, I get it but . . .

Brodie: I've started writing my essay for Constitutional and Administrative Law but it looks like hardly any of it is mine! It's all quotes and footnotes. Is that right? I wanted to look like I was bringing something new to the subject . . .

Sienna: Yeah mine's the same, it seems really disjointed when you read it because of all those references. I'm worried it's going to look like I have nothing to say.

This exchange is pretty typical of students writing their first essay at university level. It seems really alien and clunky to be constantly name-checking and attributing your content. If this worries you, take a look at any article in one of the leading journals (*Modern Law Review, Law Quarterly Review* . . .); you'll see those academic authors are doing exactly the same.

You need to focus on developing more sophisticated ways of threading what you read into your own line of argument. A good way to do this is by practising reading something complex and then trying to summarise in your own words. Certainly, reading an essay that contains a quote every other sentence can be wearisome, and implies that the student hasn't really grasped the concept being communicated.

It's worth remembering that when marking your essay, your lecturers will be looking closely at your references – they want to see the quality of your research. When you look at the mark scheme you will also see that referencing is highlighted

---

2   *Williams v Bridgeport Music, Inc* 300 FRD 120.

3   Brett Trout, 'Iowa lawyer sanctioned for plagiarism' (*BlawgIT*, 17 September 2007) http://blawgit.com/2007/09/17/iowa-lawyer-sanctioned-for-plagiarism, accessed 1 May 2015.

here – it's part of the criteria we use to decide on a grade for your work. You'd be silly to disregard this.

6.3 I UNDERSTAND, SO HOW DO I ACTUALLY DO THIS REFERENCING?

So that's why you shouldn't do it, but how do you actually signpost in your essay what information you've got from which source?

This depends on the information found in your university course handbooks – be very careful to check this. However most law schools now expect their students to follow the **OSCOLA** (Oxford University Standard for Citation of Legal Authorities) method of referencing and citation. OSCOLA is edited by the Oxford Law Faculty in consultation with the Editorial Advisory Board: a board including librarians, editors, publishers and academics.

There is a great OSCOLA guide online (www.law.ox.ac.uk/published/OSCOLA_4th_edn_Hart_2012.pdf) so I'll just go through the basics here.

Essentially every time you mention an external source you need to footnote it (in Microsoft Word via *Insert* menu), with the full reference also appearing in the bibliography at the end of your piece of work. Remember this may well add to your word count!

We'll go on to look at how you cite primary and secondary legal materials in your written work, but first it's worth looking at the case citations you may come across in your lecture notes and textbooks.

6.4 STRANGE CITATION

When you begin your law course you'll be perplexed by all the new terminology you have to learn – the bits of Latin and the meaning of legal terms. However those strange citation things will give you most grief early on. How on earth do you unpick all those initials and numbers, and what do they mean? For cases this is particularly true as there are a few odd formats once you have learnt the 'normal' ones. Here's an example of a standard law report citation:

This basically means the case you are looking for is found in Volume 2 of the *All England Law Reports* from 1984, beginning at page 54.

What might throw you a little off track is when you see something that looks like this:

[2008] EWCA Civ 1304

This is what is known as a neutral citation. It is a way of referring to a case without tying it to a commercially published series of law reports. This has only been in operation since the 2001/2002 period. When you look at the case on BAILII you'll see it has a very set format: single spacing with paragraph numbers and no page numbers. Our citation above translates as Case Number 1304 of 2008 within the England and Wales Court of Appeal Civil Division.

'I LOOKED FOR THIS ON THE SHELVES BUT COULDN'T FIND IT!'

Yes – neutral citations only really 'work' online; you would need to find where it has been reported in a series of law reports to get the print version (using, somewhat ironically, an online database or the *Current Law Case Citator* if your library has it.

Other neutral citations to look out for:

UKSC – UK Supreme Court

EWCA Crim – England and Wales Court of Appeal Criminal Division

EWHC – England and Wales High Court

Note in the High Court the EWHC abbreviation may be followed by an abbreviated division in brackets: (Ch) for Chancery, (QB) for Queens Bench, (Admin) for Administrative, (Fam) for Family, (Comm) for Commercial, (TCC) for Technology and Construction, (Admlty) for Admiralty and (Pa) for Patent.

If you see a neutral citation with a square bracketed number at the end e.g. [2008] EWCA Civ 1304 at [63], this refers to the paragraph number within that specific case.

A final example of strange citations might be seen if you are looking for much older case law. Many pre-1865 cases have dual citation: a citation in the nominate reports and one in the English Reports. A reference within the English Reports is straightforward; just being the year, volume, ER and the page number (just don't get this mixed up with the All ER). However a nominate reference looks odd as it is not always composed of initials. You'll remember from Chapter 3 on the English legal system that they are named after the reporters themselves, so they look like shortened words. Table 6.2 shows a few to illustrate what I mean:

Table 6.2 Seeing equivalent citations within the nominate reports and English reports

Nominate reference	English report reference
1 Bing. 156	130 ER 63
1 Car. & P. 174	171 ER 1150
2 Chan. Cas 104	22 ER 867
1 Kemble 891	83 ER 1303
9 M. & W. 777	152 ER 330
8 Beav. 469	50 ER 184

You can find many of these older cases on Lexis or Westlaw, but they display best on HeinOnline. Have a go at finding these old cases by citation:

6 Car. & P. 671

3 My. & Cr. 471

112 ER 1436

8 Taunt. 250

84 ER 697

Now back to OSCOLA and how you refer to primary and secondary materials within your essays.

6.4.1 Citing a case?

OSCOLA prescribes that you cite a case in the following way:

Party names | neutral citation | *Law Reports* citation | court in brackets.

Jones v Kernott [2011] UKSC 53 [2012] 1 AC 776 (SC)

Always use the 'official' version of a case from the *Law Reports* (e.g. AC, QB, Ch, Fam), as laid down in *Practice Direction: Citation of Authorities* (2012). If the case is not reported in the *Law Reports* then use the All ER or WLR, failing this then a specialist series of reports is your next best option.

Some cases will be unreported or too recent to be reported (published). In the instance of older unreported cases (before the system of neutral citation was developed) then you will have to use the most authoritative report available, sometimes this will be a (brief) report from something like the *Times Law Reports*. Remember for moot purposes you need to avoid neutral citation but cite from a reported source.

Take a look at the OSCOLA guide to see how to reference EU and European Court of Human Rights cases.

6.4.2 Citing a piece of legislation?

Acts should always be cited via the short title and relevant section/sub-section.

Human Rights Act 1998, s 8 (3)(b)

6.4.3 Citing a journal article?

Jeremy McBride, 'The Doctrine of Exclusivity and Judicial Review' [1983] 1 CJQ 268

When you need to indicate a specific page number, do so by putting a comma after the starting page number and adding the page you are pinpointing:

Jeremy McBride, 'The Doctrine of Exclusivity and Judicial Review' [1983] 1 CJQ 268, 271

6.4.4 Citing a book?

Ian Loveland, *Constitutional Law, Administrative Law, and Human Rights: A Critical Introduction* (6th edn, OUP 2012)

Jeremy Horder, *Excusing Crime* (OUP 2007)

HLA Hart, *Essays in Jurisprudence and Philosophy* (OUP: Clarendon Press, 1983)

6.4.5 Citing a chapter in an edited book?

Peter Birks, 'Misnomer' in WR Cornish (ed), *Restitution, Past, Present and Future: Essays in Honour of Gareth Jones* (Hart, 1998)

6.4.6 Citing from an encyclopedia?

Halsbury's Laws, (5th edn, 2012) vol 32, para 508

6.4.7 Citing a web resource?

This is the route for referencing any sources that you find online but that aren't published elsewhere – these might be websites or blogs.

Sometimes students get confused and think they need to mention that they got their source from a specific legal database – this isn't necessary.

Mark Elliott, 'My Analysis of the Conservative Party's Proposals for a British Bill of Rights' (*Public Law for Everyone*, 3 October 2014). http://publiclaw foreveryone.com/2014/10/03/my-analysis-of-the-conservative-partys-proposals-for-a-british-bill-of-rights/ accessed 4 October 2014.

6.4.8 Citing an online-only journal

Angela Daly, 'The AOL Huffington Post Merger and Bloggers' Rights' (2012) 3(3) EJLT http://ejlt.org/article/view/166 accessed 10 August 2014.

6.4.9 Citing a newspaper?

David Pannick, 'Give the Supreme Court Authority Over Human Rights Law' *The Times* (London, 12 June 2014) 61.

6.5 TEST YOURSELF!

Think back to Chapter 4 on legal research, where Ashwin and Brodie were busy with some research for an essay. Brodie went on to write a piece of coursework on legal accountability in relation to social media, here's an excerpt from his bibliography . . . can you spot any errors? (Then see Figure 6.1.)

Cases

Lord McAlpine of West Green v Bercow [2013] EWHC 1342 (QB)

Jeynes v News Magazines Ltd and another [2008] EWCA Civ 130 (CA)

Chambers v DPP [2013] 1 WLR 1833

Flood v Times Newspapers [2012] UKSC 11 [2012] 4 All ER 913

Chase v News Group Newspapers Ltd [2002] EWCA Civ 1772 [2003] EMLR 11 (QB)

Books

Michael Jones and Anthony Dugdale, Clerk & Lindsell on Torts (21st edn Sweet & Maxwell 2014)

Alistair Mullis and Richard Parkes, *Gatley on Libel and Slander* (2013) 12th edn Sweet & Maxwell

Legislation

Defamation Act 2013

Communications Act

Articles

'McAlpine, the Attorney General and the Defamation Act – social media accountability in 2013' (2013) 24(7) Ent LR 233

Paul Bernal, *'A defence of responsible tweeting'* (2014) 19(1)
Communications Law, 12

Lindsay McIntosh, "Teenagers jailed over riot call on facebook", The Times
(13 Dec 2011) 19

Nick Cohen, 'Where are the judges fit for the internet age?' Observer,
(London, 12 Feb 2012) 41

Gillespie, Alistair 'Twitter, jokes and the law', (2012) 76(5) J. Crim.L 364

Sarah Birkbeck, 'Can the use of social media be regulated?' (2013) 19(3)
CTLR 83

David Allen Green, 'The "Twitter Joke Trial" returns to the High Court'
(*New Statesman*, 22 June 2012) <www.newstatesman.com/blogs/
david-allen-green/2012/06/twitter-joke-trial-david-allen-green>

Brodie's mistakes!

Cases

Lord McAlpine of West Green v Bercow [2013] EWHC 1342 (QB)
Jeynes v News Magazines Ltd and another [2008] EWCA Civ 130 (CA)
Chambers v DPP [2013] 1 WLR 1833
Flood v Times Newspapers [2012] UKSC 11 [2012] 4 All ER 913
Chase v News Group Newspapers Ltd [2002] EWCA Civ 1772 [2003] EMLR 11 (QB)

Books

Michael Jones and Anthony Dugdale Clerk & Lindsell on Torts (21ˢᵗ edn Sweet &
Maxwell 2014)
Alistair Mullis and Richard Parkes, *Gatley on Libel and Slander* (2013) 12ᵗʰ edn
Sweet & Maxwell

Legislation

Defamation Act 2013
Communications Act

Articles

McAlpine, the Attorney General and the Defamation Act – social media
accountability in 2013 (2013) 24(7) Ent.L.R. 233
Paul Bernal, *'A defence of responsible tweeting'* (2014) 19(1) Communications Law,
12
Lindsay McIntosh, "Teenagers jailed over riot call on facebook", The Times (13 Dec
2011) 19
Nick Cohen, 'Where are the judges fit for the internet age?' Observer, (London, 12
Feb 2012) 41
Gillespie, Alistair, 'Twitter, jokes and the law', [2012] 76(5) J. Crim.L 364
Sarah Birkbeck, 'Can the use of social media be regulated?' (2013) 19(3) C.T.L.R.83
David Allen Green, 'The "Twitter Joke Trial" returns to the High Court' (*New
Statesman*, 22 June 2012) <http://www.newstatesman.com/blogs/david-allen-
green/2012/06/twitter-joke-trial-david-allen-green>

Callout annotations:
- Case names should always be in italics
- Missing the neutral citation and court (2012) EWHC 2157 (Admin)
- A Supreme Court case will definitely be reported in the Law Reports – always use most authoritative series. This should be (2012) 2 AC 273
- Needs to be in italics
- All the right components but in the wrong order! Should be (12th edn, Sweet & Maxwell 2013)
- Need the year – 2003
- Who is the author of this?
- No need for italics
- Single quote marks only
- Should be in italics
- Firstname, surname required
- Needs date of access at end

Figure 6.1 Brodie's mistakes

6.6 ARE THERE OTHER THINGS I CAN DO TO AVOID PLAGIARISM?

So the examples of how to cite in OSCOLA are what you would put in a footnote, but what about what you actually write within the body of the text? There are two main ways of adding the views of others into your essay: by *quoting* and by *paraphrasing*. As we mentioned in the table earlier in this chapter, both of these methods need careful attention to ensure you are not plagiarising.

So you've done your research; you've pinpointed the key cases in this area of law, you have also followed up on hints for extra reading in the lecture and tutorial handout. Happily you've found a couple of really good journal articles and also a useful part of the judgment in one of the cases. There's a monograph with a relevant chapter but you're finding the ideas a little hard to get your head around.

Quotes should be used sparingly; they can have the effect of breaking up the flow of your work if proper attention is not paid to how they are integrated. However a killer quote to back up the argument you are putting forward can be very effective.

Be careful not to fall into the trap of just littering your work with quotes; this is a very common mistake and one that indicates a lack of confidence in the subject.

Ashwin and Maisy have to prepare a few paragraphs on diversity within the judiciary for their legal writing class. Their tutor has told them they have to make an attempt to find a useful source and quote it within their work.

> *Maisy*:   This is so hard! Mine sounds really long-winded Ashwin. Look:

There are few women working as judges in the UK, even though the Constitutional Reform Act 2005 sought to increase numbers via the formation of the Judicial Appointments Commission. One researcher working in this area looked into the reasons why senior female lawyers do not become judges:

> Female lawyers who had reached partnership in magic circle firms, and who felt that their professional journey had been something of a struggle, were reluctant to begin again, and perhaps have to struggle to re-establish their credibility, in a world that they perceived to be even more antediluvian than City commercial law practice.[1]

Maisy:	How have you done yours?
Ashwin:	I tried to incorporate the quote into my text, so it wouldn't stand out as much. I found by looking at the way I phrased my paragraph I could just take a section from the quote, rather than the whole thing:

> Challenges remain if the UK is to increase diversity within the judiciary, despite the introduction of the Judicial Appointments Commission by the Constitutional Reform Act 2005. Research by Dame Hazel Genn finds that female partners within law firms rarely seek judicial office, stating that they 'were reluctant to begin again, and perhaps have to struggle to re-establish their credibility, in a world that they perceived to be even more antediluvian than City commercial law practice'.[1]

The footnote (for both) would read as follows:

1 Hazel Genn, *The Attractiveness of Senior Judicial Appointments to Highly Qualified Practitioners* (Directorate for Judicial Office, 2008).

Paraphrasing is where you put the ideas you've read into your own words. This is a great way of showing you have really got to grips with the concepts involved and want to communicate them in your own way. This takes practice, often students automatically think the words of the author or judge cannot possibly be written in another way.

Ashwin has a go at taking his paragraph one step further, by getting rid of the quote altogether. He still makes sure to give Dame Hazel credit though!

> Challenges remain if the UK is to increase diversity within the judiciary, despite the introduction of the Judicial Appointments Commission by the Constitutional Reform Act 2005. Research by Dame Hazel Genn[1] finds that female partners within law firms rarely seek judicial office, having faced so many challenges reaching such seniority within commercial law practice that the prospect of doing it all over again is unappealing.
>
> 1 Hazel Genn, *The Attractiveness of Senior Judicial Appointments to Highly Qualified Practitioners* (Directorate for Judicial Office, 2008).

6.7 FINAL THOUGHTS

Writing a piece of coursework is difficult – you need to understand the question, do the research, critically analyse the existing law and write capably. Those marks up for grabs are too precious to jeopardise by being clumsy with your referencing. In your first few weeks of university follow these top tips:

1   Print out the OSCOLA Quick Reference Guide and stick it on your wall.
2   Practice referencing cases, books, journal articles and chapters within books.
3   Pick a page from a textbook that interests you, and try putting some of the concepts into your own words – refine your paraphrasing technique!

CATCHING UP WITH OUR FRIENDS . . .

Brodie is assisting Ashwin with his moot and is a little worried about how he will refer to all these cases, both in writing and aurally. He decides to have a practice – taking one case he'll use within the assessed moot and noting how it will appear both in a moot context, and within an essay.

   Chartbrook Ltd v Permission Homes Ltd

Within a skeleton: *Chartbrook Ltd v Permission Homes Ltd* [2009] 1 AC 1101

Verbally within a moot: If I could take your Ladyship to *Chartbrook Ltd v Permission Homes Ltd*, which can be found within volume 1 of the Law Reports Appeal Cases for 2009, beginning at page 1101. You can find this within the pink tab of my bundle . . .

Whether in an essay or in a skeleton argument, you should reference cases in the usual way; the case name should be in italics followed by the citation, or you may place the citation in a footnote.

Chapter 7
Mooting and public speaking: Speaker's Corner

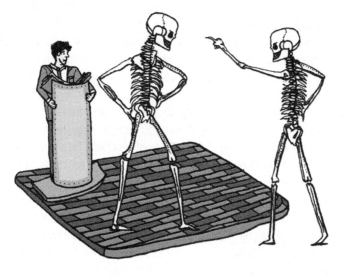

7.1 INTRODUCTION

You know you should do it but it feels so wrong. What on earth are we talking about, trying sushi for the first time, bungee jumping . . . nope it must be speaking in public just like they do in the House of Commons (yawn fest). Think you can do better than those politicians and barristers, then read and take note.

Regardless of where you see the law taking you, public speaking expertise is valued highly. Verbal reasoning is a key transferable skill, which can be used in numerous situations; you could be giving a presentation in class, putting yourself across well at an interview, networking, or in a formal setting taking the form of a debate or moot competition.

As a legal professional your voice will be all-important to you. Like in a reality TV show that involves singing, it's not all about your appearance but rather your voice that will make you stand out and get you noticed. So you need to learn how to project your voice and articulate yourself. Your voice is the tool of your trade. So like if you are like someone who likes to use the word like a lot in their sentences then like perhaps you should think about why this may hinder getting your ideas across . . . like. If you ever find us teaching you then be sure to be afraid because we shall make you repeat your sentence in front of everyone until you can do it without the dreaded word 'like' in it!

There are a number of different scenarios in which you may find yourself speaking in public. You may get involved in mooting and debating competitions, in which you will only succeed if you confidently articulate your arguments to others. You may be lucky enough to secure an assessment day with a law firm, which will involve others assessing your verbal reasoning skills, with a view to deciding if you should be offered an interview for a further interview! For those of you who like to get stuck into university life, you may put yourself forward for a position of responsibility, which will involve you representing student views at meetings with your lecturers and head of schools and let's face it; you will want to keep them on side with everything that you say. To be able to get through your degree you will have to participate in tutorials and presentations. Tutorials are the perfect environment to allow you to engage in discussion and debate with your fellow students and your lecturer. Speaking up in tutorials can be daunting but once you start engaging in discussion, your confidence will grow and your public speaking skills improve within a matter of weeks. It is therefore vital that you fully participate in your tutorials. Those of you who are thinking that you will sit strategically hiding behind a fellow student and say very little, trust us we shall expect you to talk! But let's not forget another important situation in which your public speaking skills will be put to the test, the all-important interview. If you have not taken advantage of developing your public speaking skills and thereby your verbal reasoning skills, this will, unfortunately, become apparent in interviews.

Aside from engaging in daily verbal reasoning in tutorials, competing in moot competitions is the most effective way to improve your verbal reasoning skills. Mooting requires you to think on your feet and so your ability to quickly come up with and respond to arguments becomes sharper. A moot is a fictitious case, which is being appealed and will be heard in an appellate court. The appeal is based on points of law that you have to consider, argue and present. You will be assigned a side by the moot organiser so you could be appearing either for the appellant or the respondent. There are usually two grounds of appeal and each team usually consists of a senior and a junior member. You will have to decide with your moot partner whether you will be the senior or the junior in your team, although the best way to do this is to look at the grounds of appeal and tackle the ground of appeal that you feel most comfortable with. You will then have to conduct your legal research, write a skeleton argument and prepare your submissions.

Entering into moot competitions can of course have other benefits such as networking with the professionals, enhancing your CV and perhaps winning some prize money (see Chapter 8 on employability for more examples of how to enhance your CV). As a newbie to law, mooting is one of the few ways you can do something that feels like you're practising 'being a lawyer' since a lot of the pro bono and client-facing opportunities don't become available until you have a little more law under your belt.

The rest of this chapter will focus on public speaking in the context of a moot but most of this advice applies to all public speaking scenarios.

7.2 WHY MOOT?

So why put yourself through it? The obvious benefits of entering into moot competitions include networking with the professionals, enhancing your CV and perhaps winning some much needed prize money. Your research skills will be given a thorough workout; there are so many sources to use and dense academic writing can be hard to get through – we've covered this in Chapter 4 on legal research. In mooting you might wow with your advocacy skills but without solid research into the problem, the judge will soon pick holes in your argument. What's pretty cool about researching for a moot problem is that if that subject comes up when you're sweating it out in an exam room you will be home and dry.

With regard to networking; moots are presided over by a moot judge – a role played generally by a barrister, a solicitor, a law academic or sometimes by an actual judge (see 8.6 'Take it!' for further advice on networking). These people will have given up their time to perform this role and will often be happy to stay on and chat further after the moot has ended. It's a great opportunity to make all-important contacts, with student mooters sometimes gaining chances to shadow someone in court, do some marshalling, secure a mini-pupillage or just a promise of future guidance for applications.

Whether you win or lose is not important, as potential employers will look for evidence of your participation in such competitions as it demonstrates that you have conviction in what you are saying and that they too should take note of what you have to say. *This is not to say that if you have not taken part in a moot that you will not be taken seriously in an interview, but rather that you have some experience of communicating with others in a formal setting and that you are enthusiastic about the law.* If you are lucky enough to get picked to represent your university in a national mooting competition then that demonstrates you're dedicated *and* potentially a strong advocate.

7.3 WHAT COMPETITIONS AND HOW DO YOU GET INVOLVED?

Internal competitions are usually run by your law school – they offer an opportunity to start mooting in slightly less terrifying surroundings. You may find your school has a competition just for your cohort (e.g. for the GDL course) or that there is a moot that students in all programmes can enter.

Externally there are loads of competitions your university can enter teams into. In the UK the most established competitions include the ICLR National Mooting Competition, the OUP/BPP National Mooting Competition and the ESU/Essex Court National Mooting Competition. There are also those competitions run by student societies like the National Law Student Association and the UK Law Students Association. Undergraduate students in London have the great London Universities Moot Shield (LUMS) to get involved with.

There are a number of inter-varsity moots run by universities and also by some of the Inns of Court. These are usually one-day events that operate on a knockout basis. In addition, some sets of chambers run a moot in their area of practice; for example Francis Taylor Building run a very prestigious moot in the areas of Public and European Law.

Some moot competitions pivot around one specialist area; the University of Oxford run an Intellectual Property Moot and a separate Media Law one. However, these specialist moots often take place outside the UK; there is the Vis Arbitration Moot (Vienna); the European Moot Court (Europe – location changes annually); European Human Rights Moot Court Competition (Strasbourg); and the granddaddy of them all, the Jessup International Law Moot Court Competition (USA). These moots differ tremendously from domestic competitions and demand a huge commitment, as the workload is weighty.

Universities will have different ways of picking their teams – some by skeleton argument, others by giving interested mooters five minutes to demonstrate their advocacy on a certain point. Some will automatically give a place to the winners of their internal moot competition from the previous year. For the international competitions, some universities will run an elective module on that area of law and then choose the best students to form the moot team.

7.4 MOOTING BASICS

So let's get to grips with some basic terminology that you will encounter in mooting.

Rule 52.1 of the Civil Procedure Rules helps us to explain the first five terms:

- *Appeal*: includes an appeal by way of case stated.[1]
- *Appeal Court*: the court to which an appeal is made.[2]
- *Lower Court*: the court, tribunal or other person or body from whose decision an appeal is brought.[3]
- *Appellant:* a person who brings or seeks to bring an appeal.[4]
- *Respondent*: a person other than the appellant who was a party to the proceedings in the lower court and who is affected by the appeal; and a person who is permitted by the appeal court to be a party to the appeal.[5]
- *Claimant*: the person who made the original claim.
- *Defendant*: the person who was asked to defend the original claim.
- *Ground of appeal*: the reason the appellant disagrees with the decision of the trial judge.
- *Submission*: the formal argument that you put forward on the disputed point of law. This can be both oral and written, and will be a combination of your party's reading of the law and any applicable evidence. When speaking, you may begin your arguments to the Court by stating 'We submit' or 'In our submission'.
- *Cross appeal*: where both parties are unhappy with parts of the first instance judgment and appeal on different points.

---

1 Civil Procedure Rules: Rules 52.1.
2 *Ibid* is Latin for 'in the same place' – you will see it a lot as it is traditional to use Latin when making such points.
3 *Ibid*.
4 *Ibid*.
5 *Ibid*.

- *Judicial interventions*: the occasions on which a judge at a moot will ask questions or probe deeper of a mooter.
- *Doctrine of judicial precedent*: this explains how cases relate to each other by drawing on the decisions made in the past on similar issues, i.e. if something has worked well in the past, we should follow a similar approach in the future.
- *Skeleton argument*: comprises the outline of your argument, given to the judge and your opponents prior to the moot.
- *Exchange of skeleton argument*: the occasion of exchanging an outline of your argument to the opposing side.

7.5 WHAT MAKES A GOOD MOOTER?

All moots will have slightly different judging criteria, but generally speaking you will be judged on the following:

- dress/etiquette;
- skeleton argument;
- bundle;
- dealing with judicial interventions (aka responding to questions);
- presentation of legal argument;
- content of legal argument; and
- strategy or style may also be judged in some competitions.

We'll cover all of these areas in the rest of the chapter – giving you advice on how to get the best marks, and we'll throw in some examples of what not to do!

7.6 GIVE ME THE BASICS: HOW DOES IT WORK?

People often think of mooting in relation to the event itself, but most of the work is done beforehand. First thing to happen is that you will receive your moot problem.

The moot problem will be a fictional one, which is far from cut and dried on either side. Obviously the phrase 'moot point' comes from the concept of something being able to be argued either way.

Most moot problems are situated in the appeal courts – the Court of Appeal or the UK Supreme Court. Basically speaking, the case has already happened and there has been an appeal against the earlier decision. You will either be the *appellant* – who believes the trial judge was wrong in the earlier incidence of the case and wants the decision reversed, or you will be the *respondent* who will want nothing changed and believes the trial judge to be correct.

Generally speaking there are two members in a team – the senior and the junior. In the 'real world' of the courtroom these would be termed leader and junior. The moot organiser will specify if you are to represent the appellant or the respondent.

Each moot will normally have two grounds of appeal so the senior appellant and respondent will deal with ground one, while the junior appellant and respondent tackle ground two. These will sometimes overlap when the judge asks you questions so you need to have an understanding of both grounds, regardless of your allocation. Note that some external competitions will have a different order of submissions.

7.7 WHO DOES WHAT?

7.7.1 Senior

Like the host at a party, senior counsel for the appellant must take responsibility for putting everyone at ease. They must introduce themselves, their junior and the respondent counsel, as well as giving the judge a summary of the facts within the appeal.

Senior counsel for the respondent has slightly reduced responsibilities: introducing themselves and their junior to the judge. A summary isn't required unless they feel their opposition have missed something out.

Good practice is that senior members offer the judge a summary of their submissions before stating what action they wish the court to take, and passing over to their junior.

7.7.2 Junior

Junior counsel will introduce themselves and deliver their submissions on the remaining ground. They will also be responsible for knitting together the submissions for both grounds to present to the judge, along with inviting the judge to either grant or dismiss the appeal.

7.8 PRESENTED WITH A MOOT PROBLEM

When you receive a moot problem you might want take a moment because you will probably think that you are in trouble and on the losing side. Everybody thinks this! Your opponents think this. Moots are purposely designed to challenge both of the parties competing. You will do well to remember that a barrister will read their brief and get to work thinking about how they must represent the best interests of their client rather than whether they are on the winning or losing side.

Working your way through the moot problem in a logical manner is essential. The following steps will help guide you through the moot problem.

MOOTING GUIDE

(i)   Read through the moot problem carefully. The facts and/or initial judgment may not seem favourable to you and you may start feeling like you are really up against it. Just remember, moot problems are designed to test your ability to think on your feet and articulate arguments. They are not designed to be easy, otherwise wouldn't everyone be studying law? Determine what area of law you have to deal with and what specific topic is being addressed in the problem.

(ii)   What was the decision of the lower court? What were the reasons for its decision and what legal authorities or principles were applied? These authorities and/or principles will provide you with a platform for understanding the initial decision and for preparing your legal arguments.

(iii) Which side are you on? You will be told whether you are appearing for the appellant or the respondent. You will also have to determine with your moot partner, what ground of appeal you are dealing with.

(iv)   Read through, in full, all of the legal authorities that have been relied upon to reach the decision in the lower court. The key to being a good advocate is to identify the strengths in your arguments as well as the weaknesses. Being prepared in this way will mean that you are not caught off guard in responding to judicial interventions and that you will be able to identify the strengths and weaknesses in your opponents' arguments. Consider how the authorities have been interpreted and applied; would you apply them differently?

(v)   Make a list of case law and any other relevant legal authorities.

(vi)   Start your research.
(vii) Prepare three bundles – one for yourself, one for your opponent and one for the judge.
(viii) Prepare your submission.
(ix)   Draft your skeleton argument.
(x)   Exchange your skeleton arguments.

Now we need to put these steps to the test using the following moot problem as an example:

IN THE COURT OF APPEAL

Linda Cahill
V
Bulldozer Builders

Linda Cahill decided to have some renovation work carried out on her house. Her friends recommended a company called Bulldozer Builders. Linda invited Bulldozer to quote her for the work that she wanted to have carried out. Bulldozer inspected the building and on account of this inspection, quoted Linda £50,000 for the work. Linda and Bulldozer agreed that the work would start 1 February and if the work finished by 1 June a bonus of £5,000 would be payable by Linda. Linda explained that it was her daughter's first birthday and she is hosting a big party on 11 June and needs time to set things up for the party. Bulldozer sent over their standard contract to Linda for her signature on the contract, which included the clause about the bonus payment but mistakenly unknown to both parties, the date stated was 10 June rather than 1 June. Linda signed the contract without reading it and did not notice the difference in the date.

Bulldozer duly started the building work and Linda, being so impressed with the standard of their work, asked for a quote to build a garage alongside her house. Bulldozer said that they would add that to their workload and that it would cost £7,000 although they would need this payment upfront to help pay for materials. Linda signed a new contract for the additional building work and happily paid them £7,000 in advance.

Bulldozer finished the renovations by 10 June and started work on the garage. Bulldozer asked Linda for their payment and their bonus payment. Linda refused to pay Bulldozer the bonus on account of them having missed the completion date of 1 June. Bulldozer highlighted that according to the contract that Linda had signed they were entitled to the bonus payment as they had finished their work by 10 June.

When Bulldozer were beginning to dig the foundation for the garage floor, they came across what was discovered to be an unexploded World War II bomb. Bulldozer immediately stopped their work and called the Army bomb disposal team. Bulldozer refused to build the garage as they had already spent £3,000 on materials and it would cost an additional £5,000 to complete due to the days they had lost while waiting for the bomb to be disposed of. The result would be that they would be late beginning their next contract with another party and be in breach of that contract.

Linda asked for her £7,000 to be repaid due to a total failure of consideration. Bulldozer refused to pay in accordance with the following clause in their contract:

> 3.1.1 While best endeavours will be made to complete all work, we shall not be liable for any failure of or delay in the performance of this agreement for the period that such failure or delay is due to events beyond our reasonable control, including but not limited to acts of God, war, strikes, government orders or any other *force majeure* event.

The trial judge accepted that in accordance with the principles of offer and acceptance, the relevant date by which the work was to be completed for the bonus to be payable was 10 June and that nothing outside the four corners of the contract could be used to contradict what is contained in the contract as per *L'Estrange v F Graucob Ltd* (1934) 2 KB 394.

The trial judge declined to accept Bulldozer's argument that the discovery of an unexploded World War II bomb frustrated the contract or that its discovery of the bomb falls within the scope of clause 3.1.1 and thus does not invoke the clause. In accordance with *Davis Contractors Ltd v Fareham UDC* [1956] AC 696, mere hardship or inconvenience will not frustrate the contract. In addition, a *force majeure* event must specifically be stated in a *force majeure* clause for it to be effective.

Linda appeals to the Court of Appeal on the first ground:

(i)   That the contract must be interpreted in accordance with the parties true intention which here was that a bonus payment would only be payable if the building work were to be completed by 1 June and the discussion that she had with Bulldozer should be taken into account and the agreement should be rectified to reflect the true intentions of both parties.

Bulldozer cross-appeal to the Court of Appeal on the second ground:

(ii) That the trial judge erred in applying the doctrine of frustration since it is near impossible for Bulldozer to perform their obligation under the contract and in the alternative, the trial judge interpreted clause 3.1.1 too narrowly as the discovery of the unexploded World War II bomb is an eventuality that falls within the scope of the clause and the contract is therefore frustrated.

7.9 WORKING THROUGH A MOOT PROBLEM

7.9.1 Read though the moot problem carefully

Reading through this moot problem, you should be able to identify the following things:

- *Who are the parties?*

    - They are Linda Cahill and Bulldozer Builders.

- *Who is the appellant and the respondent?*

    - With respect to the *first* ground of appeal, Linda is the appellant as the decision in the lower court went against her and she would like this part of the decision to be reversed. Bulldozer are the respondent.
    - With respect to the *second* ground of appeal, Bulldozer are the appellant as the decision in the lower court went against them and they would like this part of the decision to be reversed. Linda is therefore the respondent.

- *What area of law is relevant and what specific issues?*

    - You should be able to identify with ease that this moot problem involves contract law. You can gauge the specific area of law being addressed from the grounds of appeal. As you can see from the grounds of appeal, you will be given a few hints as to what line of argument you should follow, but a hint is all it is, because it is for you to conduct thorough legal research to come up with persuasive arguments to achieve the result that the party you are representing would like. It might be helpful at this stage for you to draw a mind map with all of these questions in mind. What is essential is that you need to consider both parties' position and potential arguments. Do not fall into the trap of thinking that you only need to know the arguments for your party. A good mooter or indeed a good advocate should be able to predict his or her opponent's arguments and next move in order to highlight weaknesses in their argument before they even get a chance to convince the judge otherwise.

- *Why is there an appeal?*

  - Linda is appealing because she believes that the conversation that she and Bulldozer had represents the true intention of the parties and that there has simply been a drafting error resulting in a mistake in their agreement. The problem that Linda faces is that she has signed the contract and therefore she is taken to have read the contract. A word to the wise, always read the small print!
  - Bulldozer are appealing because they believe that the clause in the contract with regard to the garage covers the eventuality that materialised, which has made it difficult for them to build the garage. They therefore believe that the contract provides for this risk arising or in the alternative that the principles of frustration apply.

- *What is the reason for the decision?*

  - The reason for the decision for the first ground is Linda signed the contract and is therefore taken to have read and agreed to all of the contents in the contract.
  - The reason for the decision for the second ground is that the discovery of the World War II bomb was not covered in clause 3.1.1 and therefore it is thought not to apply. The doctrine of frustration is not applied because it is not impossible to perform the contract but rather more expensive and time-consuming.

- *What is each party seeking?*

  - Linda would like the Court of Appeal to grant her the equitable remedy of rectification to rectify the mistake in the agreement.
  - Bulldozer would like the doctrine of frustration to apply or in the alternative; they would like a much broader interpretation of clause 3.1.1,

which would relieve them from performing their obligations under the contract to build a garage for Linda.

- *In what court will the case be heard?*

    – You probably learnt about the doctrine of judicial precedent and court hierarchy in the first week or two of your degree. Did you see it as a means to an end? If so how wrong you were! A reason why you learn this so early on and why it appears in so many books such as this one is that it is the foundation for understanding how the common law develops and understanding by what authorities the court, in which the case is being heard, is restricted. So, for example, here the case will be heard in the Court of Appeal so it is bound by decisions of the Supreme Court or the House of Lords and by its own previous decisions subject to three exceptions established in *Young v Bristol Aeroplane Co Ltd* [1944] KB 718 (CA) (see Table 3.1).

7.9.2 What was the decision of the lower court and how to start preparing your arguments?

You may look at moot problems such as this one and feel a little terrified because you do not know where to start. Do you start reading all of your contract law textbooks from start to finish hoping that you miraculously come across the relevant area that this moot problem happens to be dealing with or do you conduct a Google search hoping that someone somewhere has posted up help on this very moot problem? Sadly neither of these options is efficient and nor are they likely to help you formulate your submissions. What you need to do is to understand and appreciate the reason for the decision in the lower court. It is only when you do this that you can start identifying key terms that you need to start your research and not end up on a wild goose chase.

Starting with the first ground of appeal, the reason for the decision is Linda signed the contract and is therefore taken to have read and agreed to all of the contents in the contract. In this instance you are fortunate enough to have been given two hints that will help you to understand the reasons behind the lower court's decision. You have been provided with some key terms and an authority that the court used. Sometimes you will not be provided with an authority at all, which is not to say that the court did not use one, but rather it is not included in the moot problem. The rules of the moot competition in which you are participating will state how many authorities you can rely on in making your submissions. So, how do you begin your research? Start by highlighting key terms and any authorities used. So, for example, here you could highlight the terms:

- Standard contract
- Signature
- *L'Estrange v F Graucob Ltd*
- Mistakenly

These terms and authority should give you a clue that the ground of appeal concerns the situation when one party signs a contract that contains a mistake, which they are asking to be rectified. You should then look up the rules on mistake in contract in your textbook. This will be your starting position only because as we all know textbooks are a secondary source of law and merely the beginning of your research path (see Chapter 3 for more advice on secondary sources). You should then read in full, yes in full, any authorities that the lower court has used to reach its decision, which in this case is the case of *L'Estrange v F Graucob Ltd*. In this process, note down any points that are pertinent either for you or your opponent. A good mooter and a good teammate for that matter would also make notes of any points that are useful for their moot partner too!

The reason for the decision for the second ground is that the doctrine of frustration does not apply because it is not impossible to perform the contract but rather more expensive and time consuming. The second reason that is given is that the discovery of the World War II bomb was not covered in clause 3.1.1 and therefore is thought not to apply to this situation.

So the hints that you have been given here are that this ground of appeal relates to frustration of contract and you have been given the name of a case on which the lower court has relied. There is, however, a second part to this ground of appeal, which is that the discovery of the bomb is not covered within the scope of clause 3.1.1. We are told that this is a very narrow interpretation. So what terms or authority should you highlight for this ground of appeal?

- Frustration
- *Davis Contractors Ltd v Fareham UDC*
- Interpretation
- Scope
- *Force majeure*

Similarly, you ought to start reading up on the relevant area of law, which here is frustration and again, read any cases that the lower court has relied upon in full. In this instance, the case relied upon is that of *Davis Contractors Ltd v Fareham UDC*. What is slightly tricky here is that we are presented with two alternative arguments. The second reason for the decision relating to this ground of appeal is that the discovery of the World War II bomb does not fall within the scope of clause 3.1.1, which is the *force majeure* clause. This obviously is a source of contention and thus a moot point. This provides you with a lead for where to begin your research. You should at this point be thinking, might the judge have interpreted the clause too narrowly and what exactly are the rules on interpretation of contract clauses?

7.9.3 Which side are you on?

The moot organiser will inform you as to whether you are to appear on behalf of the respondent or the appellant. It is then down to you and your moot partner to determine which ground of appeal each of you will deal with. The best advice that we can give you here is that you should each play to your strength. So if your moot partner is confident in dealing with vitiating factors such as mistake, then it makes sense to let your moot partner deal with ground one whether or not you are confident in dealing with ground two. Alternatively, if the area of law is completely new to both of you, then to select your ground of appeal, you may as well flip a coin! Remember, you are not competing against each other; rather this should be an example of when you are able to work in a team. Employers look for evidence of teamwork, which is considered to be an essential skill, so when you are filling out an application form and updating your CV, be sure to note this experience as an example of team work (see Chapter 8 on employability).

7.9.4 Research

7.9.4.1 Getting to grips with the legal authorities you have been given

A good starting point for your research of a moot problem is to look for the clues that you have been given. When you and your moot partner sit down, you should have a brainstorm about the moot problem and determine what subject area the moot is dealing with, and then what specific topic in that area. You should work together on the whole moot problem as far as you can before conducting your research on the ground of appeal that you have been allocated.

So where would you begin in researching for a moot problem? As a lawyer you need to develop your *communication skills* and sometimes work with some irksome people that you would otherwise like to avoid (think of all those charming individuals on a popular TV show who compete to go into business with a successful entrepreneur).

Note that this is another essential skill that employers will be looking out for. You may want to think about what would happen if you were asked in an interview about an instance of when you worked with someone you did not like and how you did not let that fact get in the way of working in a team to achieve the best result (see Chapter 8 on employability for further advice on how to prepare for interviews).

(i)   Spend some time reading through the moot problem together and figure out the area of law and the specific topics within that area (see above). This should not take you longer than an afternoon.

(ii)   Set a realistic deadline by which each of you should have completed the research for your ground of appeal.

(iii) Start by using research materials that are familiar to you. So we know that ground (i) of this moot problem is to do with contract law, particularly agreement mistake and the case of *L'Estrange*. You should then go straight ahead and pick up your edition of R. Stone's *Contract Law* and read the extract and/or commentary on *L'Estrange* and read the chapter on mistake! Read your lecture notes on the same issues. This initial research process will help you to have many 'light-bulb' moments but probably an equal number of 'bang your head on the table' moments. After this initial process, you will end up with a sense of direction for your broader research. The legal encyclopedia *Halsbury's Laws* is also a good starting point for research in a specific area. You can access this via LexisLibrary if those sexy brown volumes don't adorn the shelves of your law library.

(iv)   With regard to ground (ii) we are already told that the moot point concerns frustration and interpretation of the *force majeure* clause so there's your starting point – read up on frustration of contract and interpretation of contract clauses.

Maisy (senior appellant) reads through her lecture notes and finds that ground (i) is not like any cases that she has come across in her lectures. She then reads the chapter on mistake and looks up the case of *L'Estrange* and realises that this is an issue concerning the contents or the formation of a written contract, which contains a mistake. She then reads that once a contract is signed its contents are binding as per the decision in *L'Estrange*. However, her reading of the chapter on mistake, alerts her to a remedy called rectification, which is sometimes permitted when there is an error of the clerical type appearing in the written contract. She is starting to see both sides of the argument . . .

Brodie (junior appellant) reads through his lecture notes and uses his textbook. He starts to form the impression that the contract cannot be frustrated so there is little scope for argument but becomes a little confused – surely then this point would not be appealed? As for the alternative argument, he reads that the specific event in question must be included in the *force majeure* clause otherwise the clause may not be effective. Brodie is starting to slump, thinking that he is on the losing side . . . He has a vague recollection that there may be other sources, apart from his textbook, which might help him unpick all this, and goes to his law librarian Emily for help. She suggests he use more in-depth academic works like *Treitel* and a practitioner book called *Chitty on Contracts*. Déjà vu! Brodie vaguely remembers his lecturer Sanmeet discussing the importance of different sources like this in an induction lecture. The penny is starting to drop . . .

(v)   Once you have started to form an impression of the potential arguments that could be made for your ground of appeal, you need to develop and build on your research by upgrading your sources of law. So for example, Maisy and Brodie should refer to practitioner textbooks to formulate and develop their arguments. Some good sources to use here are Peel, *Treitel: The Law of Contract* and *Chitty on Contracts*.

(vi) A further upgrade in your research is to use case law, which is a primary source of law and your most potent weapon (see 3.7 'Case law: primary source' for more details on primary sources of law in the ELS). In your moot competition you will often be told upon how many authorities you may rely. This is often no more than three but can be up to eight in the bigger competitions; ensure you check the competition rules. An important skill to develop through mooting is selecting your resources carefully. So if you know that you can only rely on three cases, they have to support your argument to the extent that it leaves very little room for argument from your opponents.

Ashwin and Sienna are talking about how they are going to go about researching for the moot. Sienna tells Ashwin that she has already looked up the case of *Syncora Guarantee Inc. v. EMC Mortgage Corporation* Slip Copy, 2012 WL 2326068 SDNY, 19 June 2012, which is a case in support of the proposition that the court will give effect to the intention of the contract parties as found in the language used in the contract, through a quick Google search. Ashwin takes a breath and points out to Sienna that while that case may be helpful to those living in America; it is not applicable to their moot problem since they need to use English law! Ashwin reminds Sienna to pay attention to the rules that they have learnt in their Legal Skills module and to use the proper legal databases that will help them conduct their research more efficiently.

There's absolutely nothing wrong with using a search engine like Google to search for all kinds of things. Law included. We are sure most students will often start here for case summaries or definitions before progressing to the legal databases. However you must be smart about the sources you look at – plucking information from this vast sea of unregulated content can leave you at risk of using inaccurate or blatantly wrong information. You're going to stand up and moot your little heart out; getting the law wrong will ensure you lose the moot however good your advocacy.

KEY SKILLS:

- teamwork
- communication
- research
- time management.

A top mooter needs more in their armoury than Google, Wikipedia and student textbooks. Check out our chapter on research for more information on this (see Chapter 4).

7.9.5 The research steps for Ground One

Both the senior appellant and respondent will be dealing with Ground One. If you've been given cases in the moot problem – this is a great starting point. Go and look them up and read in full. For this ground this is the case of *L'Estrange v F Graucob Ltd* (1934) 2 KB 394.

Looking this up via a database will mean you can see both a summary (helpful to get you started on understanding the principles within the case) and the full text. Looking at the case in full is essential for a moot as the judge is very likely to ask you a question on any part of it – if you are using an authority (aka case) you need to know it inside out. Within a database like LexisLibrary or Westlaw you will also be able to get recommendations on journal articles to read – although you wouldn't often use a secondary source within a moot, they are useful for improving your understanding of any difficulties within a case (see Chapter 3).

To find the relevant bit within your textbook, use the Table of Cases (usually at the front of the book).

By looking within a database we can see *L'Estrange* is still very much 'good law' – being cited in other cases as recently as 2013. Looking at the facts we can see that the situations are on the face of it similar – in this 1934 case the buyer (a café owner) of a cigarette vending machine signed the contract without reading it and then objected to some exclusions in the small print when the machine turned out to be defective. Today this situation would have been dealt with via the Unfair Contract Terms Act 1977 (UCTA). However, in this case the seller was aware of the text, even if the buyer was not – for Linda and Bulldozer as neither of them was aware of the date change in the contract. *L'Estrange* doesn't seem to help us much as the principle here was that a person signing a contractual document is bound by its terms, the reading of them is immaterial. So where to go next?

Let's take a look at one of the key practitioner books in this area and see if it gives us another path to explore. One of the keywords we picked out from the problem was 'mistake' – we're interested in how other cases have dealt with mistake in a written contract.

Looking at *Treitel: The Law of Contract*, we find Chapter 8 on mistakes includes something called rectification, which sounds like some form of remedy.[6] In a discussion on the types of mistake (8–60) we find:

> An obvious drafting mistake may be corrected as a matter of construction, provided there was a clear mistake on the face of the instrument and it is also clear what correction ought to be made in order to cure the mistake.

Several cases are footnoted here and will probably be helpful to us – *East v Pantiles (Plant Hire)* (1981) 263 EG 61 and *Chartbrook Ltd v Persimmon Homes Ltd* [2009] 1 AC 1101. *Treitel* suggests that a claim for construction might be successful here – *East* confirms that a contract should be construed in the manner intended where there is a clear mistake on the face of the instrument AND where it is clear what correction is required.

Moving on to use *Chitty* we look up *Chartbrook* in the Table of Cases to find where it has been mentioned in the text. There are several references under Rectification of Written Terms (5–113) and others within Chapter 12 on Construction of Terms (12–55).[7] Here we learn about the importance of context and background when interpreting contract terms, and what might be the effect when the literal meaning would be absurd – this is important considering Linda's need for time to set up for her daughter's party.

If we can't convince the judge on construing the clause in our favour then we need to have an alternative to present in the form of rectification. In the introduction to this subject within *Chitty* (5–110) we find reference to the case of *Agip SpA v Navigazione Alta Italia SpA* [1984] 1 Lloyd's Rep. 353 and a very useful description of this remedy:

> [T]he remedy of rectification is one permitted by the Court, not for the purpose of altering the terms of the an agreement entered into between two parties, but for that of correcting a written instrument which, by a mistake in verbal expression, does not accurately reflect their true agreement.

Reading further we find that the conditions for rectification are set out clearly in *Swainland Builders Ltd v Freehold Properties Ltd* [2002] 2 EGLR 71 – we need to address each of these conditions in relation to the mistake in the written contract between Linda and Bulldozer.

---

6   Edwin Peel, *Treitel: The Law of Contract* (14th edn, Sweet & Maxwell 2015).
7   Hugh Beale, *Chitty on Contracts* (32nd edn, Sweet & Maxwell 2015).

ACTIVITY

Make sure you know what each of the practitioner texts are for your core modules!

Some will be on the shelves in your law library; others may be available online via databases like LexisLibrary and Westlaw. In the library you will see them on the shelves looking imposing – leather-bound in very drab colours. Remember for lawyers these books are akin to a bible for each area of practice. FACT: criminal lawyers sleep with *Archbold* under their pillow.

7.9.6 The research steps for Ground Two

As above – you have been given a case so use this as your starting point – *Davis Contractors Ltd v Fareham UDC* [1956] AC 696. Use your textbook, the legal databases and practitioner text to find out more as above.

Remember that the research skills you're using for mooting will come in handy for assessments in other modules you are studying. You would use these same skills in researching for any essay or problem question.

7.9.7 Skeleton arguments

A skeleton argument (or 'skelly') is basically an outline of your argument and has several purposes; it:

- acts as the framework for your argument;
- allows the judge to feel secure in where you're taking him/her; and
- lets your opponents know roughly the path you're travelling.

What can be tricky is getting the balance right between spelling out your argument but not giving too much away. It should be a brief summary of the points – don't get sucked into making it feel like your actual oral submission (your speech).

Structure is key: each point should either make a proposition of law, a skeleton point in relation to the facts of the case or a conclusion you are inviting the court to draw. Always ask yourself – what are my basic submissions of law or fact? Full paragraphs are far too wordy; make a general point and then add the detail in sub-sections underneath.

IN THE COURT OF APPEAL

BETWEEN

Linda Cahill   Appellant

- AND -

Bulldozer Builders
                                Respondent

Senior Appellant's Skeleton Argument

Introduction

> This is a clear and concise introduction which sets the scene and tells the judge exactly what each party is seeking.

1. The appellant claims the contract between her and the respondents was drafted under a common mistake and that a bonus sum was only to be paid to the respondents if they completed their work by 1st June and not 10th June as stated in the contract.

2. The respondents are seeking to take advantage of their drafting error contained in the contract to the detriment of the appellant.

3. The appellant contends that the contract can be corrected either as a matter of construction or through the remedy of rectification.

> Each legal argument is signposted and divided clearly into its own section which helps all parties but particularly the judge, follow your argument.

Construction

4. The case of *East v Pantiles (Plant Hire) Ltd* (1981) 263 EG 61 confirmed that where there is a clear mistake on the face of the instrument and where it is clear what correction is required to correct the mistake, the contract should be construed in the manner intended. As a matter of construction alone, the mistake can be corrected for the following reasons:

    4.1 As a matter of construction, there has been a clerical error and the term should be construed to read 1st June. The appellant made clear to the defendant that she was hosting a party on 11th June and would like her house to be ready by 1st June to allow her time to prepare.

    4.2 The parol evidence rule does not apply here as context and background are essential in interpreting a contract as confirmed in *Chartbrook Ltd v Persimmon Homes Ltd* [2009] UKHL 38. The context here is that the appellant would only pay the bonus if she had time to prepare her house for the party.

    4.3 The mistake here is obvious and prior oral agreement for the date of completion for the bonus to be payable was reached. The literal meaning is illogical. It makes little sense for the appellant to pay a bonus payment if the renovation work is only completed a day before her daughter's party.

Rectification

> The second argument is also signposted.

5. An alternative avenue to correct the mistake is through the remedy of rectification. The case of *Agip SpA v Navigazione Alta Italia SpA (The Nai Genova and The Nai Superba)* [1984] 1 Lloyd's Rep. 353 confirmed that the remedy of rectification is available for correcting a written instrument which, by a mistake does not accurately reflect the true agreement between the parties.

6. The requirements for rectification as set out in *Swainland Builders Ltd v Freehold Properties Ltd* [2002] 2 E.G.L.R 71 are met as in prior discussions it was agreed that the work should be completed by 1st June for the bonus payment to become payable.:

    3.1. Both parties had a common continuing intention with respect to the date for completion which would require the bonus payment to be made.

    3.2. There was an outward expression of accord.

    3.3. The intention continues at the time of the execution of the contract.

    3.4. It is a mistake that the contract does not reflect the common intention.

> It is made clear, what the party is requesting from the court.

7. The court should grant the remedy of rectification as both parties were operating under a common mistake.

> This skeleton is clearly laid out and will assist the judge see this side of the argument.

Figure 7.1 Example of a good skeleton argument

Remember the skeleton is your guide; a good mooter will refer the judge to their skeleton throughout their oral submissions – using it to signpost the progress of their argument. This gives the impression to the judge that you are in control and organised, and gives them a sense of security – they hopefully feel in good hands!

Ashwin prepares his skeleton argument for his moot (see Figure 7.1).

Sienna is cautious when writing her skeleton argument in that she does not want to give the game away and prefers to be coy (see Figure 7.2).

IN THE COURT OF APPEAL

BETWEEN

Linda Cahill	**Appellant**	The introduction does not reveal very much more than the ground of appeal so it does not add anything to the argument that Sienna is trying to make.
- AND -		
Bulldozer Builders		
	Respondent	

Junior Appellant's Skeleton Argument

Introduction

1. The appellants for this ground contend that the contract to build the garage has been frustrated and/or the discovery of the unexploded World War two bomb falls within the ambit of the *force majeure* clause contained in the contract.

> Blunt way of putting forward the submission; a mention of what frustration is and why it applies to this situation would be appropriate

Frustration

2. Frustration can be applied to this situation because there has been a change in circumstances and the performance of the contract will be more onerous for Bulldozer (*Bank Line Ltd v Arthur Capel   & Co* [1919] AC 435).

> Case is stated in passing without clearly demon-strating how Sienna will seek to rely on the case.

3. As per the Law Reform (Frustrated Contracts) Act 1943, s 1(2), the appellants are entitled to retain the payment made in   advance of the contract.

Force Majeure Clause

4. Clause 3.1.1., the *force majeure* clause, expressly covers such a situation arising and therefore the appellants are not responsible for the failure to build the garage.

5. The contract should apply the doctrine of frustration and/or interpret the *force majeure* clause broadly so that the discovery of the unexploded World War II bomb falls within its scope.

> Sienna has hinted at the argument that she would like to make, but she has not explained the point here which is that the appellants have incurred expenses and the advance payment will help to meet those expenses.

 Overall this skeleton does not shed much light on what argument Sienna is seeking to make and will not help the judge see her side of the argument.

Figure 7.2 Example of a bare bones skeleton argument

7.9.8 Forget about the trees

Once the skeleton is drafted your last big task before the big day is compiling your bundle. The bundle is pivotal at the moot – almost like an extension of you. The bundle has to contain a copy of each authority you are relying upon, as well as the moot problem and your skeleton argument. So what should the ideal bundle be?

- *Smart*: use a ring binder.
- *Well organised*: total no-brainer, but you have to use tabs so that you can use a separate tab for each authority.
- *Sober*: it should look professional and weighty, avoid frivolous use of highlighter pens.

Some moots will insist on the bundle being numbered, which means a tedious trawl through your bundle individually numbering each page sequentially. Check the rules carefully.

7.9.8.1 Here are some answers to questions we know you will be thinking about

DOES IT MATTER WHICH VERSION OF THE CASE I USE IN MY SKELETON/BUNDLE?

Yes! Ordinarily most of the cases you use will be reported, which means they have been published in a physical law report that you could find in a volume on a library shelf. Lots of students are unsure about the hierarchy that exists in law reports – more on this in our chapter on sources of law (see Chapter 3) – but for mooting try to avoid using any neutral citation. These are the ones that look like this:

[2001] EWCA Civ 12 or [2009] UKSC 1 or [2013] ECWA Crim 56

This is just a way of being able to cite a case without tying it to a published source. In mooting (as it would be in practice) you need to use the case of highest authority. This was laid down in 2012 in Practice Direction: Citation of Authorities:

5. When authority is cited, whether in written or oral submissions, the following practice should be followed.

6. Where a judgment is reported in the Official Law Reports (AC, QB, Ch, Fam) published by the Incorporated Council of Law Reporting for England and Wales, that report must be cited. These are the most authoritative reports; they contain a summary of the argument. Other series of reports and official transcripts of judgment may only be used when a case is not reported in the Official Law Reports.

So if you find this useful case in a legal database and these are your options . . .

[2010] UKSC 42; [2011] 1 AC 534; [2010] 3 WLR 1367; [2011] 1 All ER 373;
[2010] 2 FLR 1900; [2010] 3 FCR 583; [2010] Fam Law 1263; (2010) 107(42)
LSG 18; (2010) 160 NLJ 1491; (2010) 154(40) SJLB 37; Times, October 22,
2010

You wouldn't go for the neutral citation [2010] UKSC 42 but preferably something
from the Official Law Reports, which would appear as QB, Ch or as in this case, AC.
The Weekly Law Reports (WLR) and All England Law Reports (All ER) are fine as a
second choice.

What is important when it comes to printing out your case for a bundle is that you
print out the right version, in the right format. It needs to look like the original in
the printed book – in an attractive font and labelled paragraphs. Usually in legal
databases you can get this version by clicking on the PDF icon rather than just
trying to print what is on your computer screen.

DO I HAVE TO PRINT OUT THE WHOLE CASE/ACT?

The answer is yes! As mentioned earlier there is no worse feeling than when the
judge wants to ask you about something later in the case and you've only printed
off the section you've quoted from. Don't be caught out! It may cost a bomb in
printing and feel like you're personally responsible for deforestation but it is
necessary here. It may be possible to ask your institution to help you out a bit as
they may be willing to do the printing for you – it's always worth a try!

GET TO KNOW YOUR BUNDLE

You might feel a bit of an idiot but you really do need to get friendly with your
bundle. You need to practise taking the judge to different parts of it – make sure
you know how to verbalise all those citations:

> If I might take your Lordship to Tab 3 in the appellant's bundle you will find the
> case of Radmacher and Granatino, reported in volume 1 of the 2011 Law
> Reports Appeal Cases beginning at page 534 . . .

When the nerves kick in at the moot you don't want to be struggling to find the
right terminology – practice will help this just become second nature.

HOW MANY BUNDLES DO I NEED?

At least two: one for you and one for the judge. It is polite to provide one to your opponents too; we have been at many moots where this doesn't happen and it looks rude and causes problems when there is a right of reply.

If you progress significantly in a moot competition, often there will be multiple judges at a semi-final and final. Don't forget they will need a bundle each – you don't want to irritate them even before the moot has begun.

7.9.9 The speech

Writing out what you are going to say is difficult. You need to get it down on paper in full to practise – and you will need to practise – delivering your oral submission to your mum, your flatmates, the dog . . . anyone who will listen.

However, what you actually use on the day is a different story. Having your whole speech in front of you may be unwieldy; it often makes your speech more stilted and monotonous. Reading slavishly from a script will make it very difficult for you to maintain solid eye contact with the judge. You want the judge to be engaged by what you are saying, not lulled to sleep. The other issue to bear in mind is that the judge will make it impossible for you to stand there and read out a script. His questions may force you to take your points out of sequence, or indeed go completely off-piste. You need to be flexible and obliging and be confident enough to jump around your submissions if required.

Flash cards with separate points on each may help to split up your speech into chunks and make your delivery more flexible.

7.9.9.1 Don't be distracting

Another reason to practise in front of people is to iron out any funny habits or quirks you may be unknowingly displaying. Common ones are as follows:

- *Too much hand action*: people like to be expressive with their hands when speaking, but in mooting this just looks messy and informal. Settle on a pose and stick to it. You might wish to keep your hands behind your back, or if there is a lectern you can rest your hands on this. Beware of looking like you're gripping on for dear life though!
- *Resist the casual 'hand in pockets' look*: it's scruffy and looks like you don't care enough.

- *Constantly unbuttoning and buttoning up jacket*: this is extremely distracting and trumpets your nerves to the judge loud and clear.

7.9.9.2 Be persuasive

To persuade someone that your argument is the right one to follow, you need to encourage them to see your side of the argument. This is a difficult skill to master and one that will only come with time and practice. It might surprise you to know that you probably practise being persuasive in your daily life. So think about the last time that your parents told you that you spent too much money on clothes or your phone bill, did you respond by agreeing with them or did you say why it was necessary to spend so much because of a pressing need? Well that is an example of trying to be persuasive, although we suspect you may not have been very convincing! Using evidence, facts and examples to support your arguments will always be more likely to persuade someone to see your side of the argument. This of course then means that you have to have carried out thorough research on the topic in question and identified the pertinent point that could support your position.

7.9.10 Key phrases

Mooting is a strange business when it comes to language – a lot of the vocabulary sounds alien, or at least makes you feel like you should be wearing an Elizabethan ruff. When writing your speech you'll need to utilise some of those listed below, but also it's imperative that you have a ready ammo of phrases to roll out as necessary. This is especially useful when the judge has just dismissed one of your submissions! If you are the senior appellant you'll need a set phrase to introduce yourself and the other three mooters. Some of these phrases can sound like you're 'sucking up' to the judge and indeed that is what is expected!

General points to note are that the court is not interested in your personal opinion. Never say 'I think . . . '. It should always be 'In my submission . . .' or 'We respectfully submit that . . .'.

7.9.10.1 Opening the moot (Senior Appellant)

May it please your Lordship, I am Emily Allbon, appearing on behalf of the Appellant, with my learned Junior Maisy Davies. My learned friend Sanmeet Dua will appear on behalf of the Respondent, along with her Junior Ashwin Clarke . . .

7.9.10.2 Establishing if the judge wants to know more about a case

'Is your Lordship familiar with the facts of this case?'

7.9.10.3 Referring to authorities

'If I could take your Lordship to tab 5, page 21; this is the case of X v Y.'

'If I can direct your Lordship's attention to X v Y found in the first volume of the Appeal Cases for 2011, at page 21 . . .'

'I respectfully adopt the opinion of HH Judge Simons in X v Y, which is at tab 3 of the bundle . . .'

7.9.10.4 Dealing with judicial interventions

'I'm grateful for your assistance my Lord, and I apologise for not having expressed myself clearly'.

'I hadn't intended to deal with that point my Lord, it is not a ground of appeal, however I am more than happy to . . .'

'My Lord, I had intended to address a different point with this authority, but should your Lord wish to hear argument on this . . .'

'Indeed my Lord, that is true for X v Y, though I would submit that the present case can be distinguished on the facts.'

Bear in mind that many of these phrases can be useful when trying to buy time in order to answer the judge more fully.

Don't be afraid to disagree with the judge – they like to see a robust (but polite) comeback, start with something like: 'My Lord, the point is a good one, however . . .'. Be sure to never interrupt though.

7.9.10.5 Running out of time?

'I am mindful of the time my Lord . . .'

'I am conscious of the time my Lord, so I will press on to my next submission unless I can assist further on this point.'

7.9.10.6 Finishing your submission

'Unless I can be of further assistance . . . those are my submissions.'

or

'Unless I can help the court any further, these are my submissions.'

ACTIVITY

What is wrong with these?

(a) I think, my Lord, that . . .
(b) It is clear from R versus Dica my Lord, reported in the England and Wales Court of Appeal Criminal Division in 2004, starting at page 1103 . . .
(c) Wonderful. Thank you my Lord.

---

1   The judge doesn't want to hear your opinion! Always use 'We submit' or 'It is our submission . . .'.
2   Two errors here: *R v Dica* would be pronounced 'The Crown and Dica'. Also remember not to use neutral citations; the [2004] EWCA Crim 1103 just means it was heard in the England and Wales Court of Appeal Criminal Division, and that it was case number 1103 of 2004. Always use the most authoritative reported case – this would be [2004] QB 1257 here ('. . . reported in the Law Reports Queens Bench Division of 2004, beginning at page 1257').
3   Acknowledge something the judge says with a simple 'I'm grateful' or 'I am obliged'. Try to resist lapsing into 'thank you'.

7.9.11 Competitiveness at a moot

However polite the language, you are still essentially trying to beat your 'learned friends' and win the moot. There will always be an element of competition but it should also be enjoyable – it's a chance to meet other law students and find out about their course and university, as well as what they're aiming to do in their career. When teams start attempting tactics and being stand-offish it all gets a bit distasteful. Judges want to hear what *you* have to say, they're not generally that interested in you constantly sniping at the other side. When referring to the other side's argument it is best to tone down your language – don't refer to their points as 'absurd' or 'ridiculous', far better to suggest that their argument might be 'difficult to sustain in the light of later authorities' or 'inconsistent with what I submit is the clear wording of the statute'. Be sure to stay at the end of the moot to talk to the other team, no matter how you are feeling.

7.9.12 How to look good mooting

Common sense prevails here and really this section should be largely redundant. Your aim is to look professional, smart and business-like, not distinctive in any way. The men among you should be wearing a white shirt along with a dark suit, tie and polished shoes. Ladies, a suit or skirt/top combo is absolutely fine. The key is to not stand out: discreet and demure. Definitely no bling!

Take note of the points raised under 7.9.9 'The speech' earlier in this chapter – looking good is about the judge being able to focus on what you're saying, not being distracted by your radical clothing or constant fidgeting. Stand up straight and look engaged.

7.9.13 Look into my eyes

You need to ensure the judge is following your argument keenly, and maintaining eye contact is pivotal to this. Your eyes should only be flicking down occasionally to your notes, which is why it is not advisable to be heavily reliant on a speech. That said; don't make the judge feel like they're in an uncomfortable intense staring competition!

7.9.14 Modes of address

You need to take careful note of which court you are mooting in, as this will dictate how you address your judge. Generally speaking you will be either in the Court of Appeal or the Supreme Court and thankfully the way you address the judge here is identical: 'My Lord' for a male judge and 'My Lady' for a female judge. When referring to them in the third person you would add '. . . ship' on the end. For example when coming to an impasse in your submission and the judge clearly isn't on board, you could say 'If your Lordship isn't with me on this matter, I will move onto my second submission . . .'.

It sounds ridiculous but it is easy to be thrown off if your judge is a different gender than you were expecting. One of our teams once was in a moot where the opposite side continuously referred to the judge as 'My Lord', despite her being a woman. Alas even this glaring error failed stop them winning. Robbed? Yep.

Outside a moot and in court, there are different terms of address for each level of court and most barristers would have a story about where they have slipped up and irritated the judge. In the High Court the address is different depending on whether the judge is a Circuit or District judge.

7.9.15 Saying it right

Knowing what to call everyone is one thing, *how* you say it is quite another. As with much of mooting it is about balance:

- Be confident but not aggressive or pompous.
- In terms of volume, think of Goldilocks and the three bears – not too quiet, not too loud but 'just right'.
- Be respectful but don't be a sycophant (suck up too much).
- Keep it simple – you will impress far more by putting your points across in a measured straightforward way than by littering your speech with overly complex words and Latin terminology.
- Resist rushing through your submissions – far better to cover one part well than garble the whole lot and the judge only retain a small percentage of it. Not too fast but not so slow that it makes the judge impatient.
- Be clear and be concise if you want to impress.

ACTIVITY

Practice explaining legal concepts or the legal significance of key cases in simple terms to your non-law friends or parents (you may need to bribe them!). Try the following to get you started:

- *caveat emptor*
- *mens rea*
- *promissory estoppel*

7.9.16 At the moot: where to sit

The easiest way to remember where to grab a seat is by thinking of the parties in the moot problem; the appellants are always the first party named and as such it is the appellants who take the seats on the left-hand side, respondents on the right. Senior Counsel are seated nearest the centre of the room (see Figure 7.3).

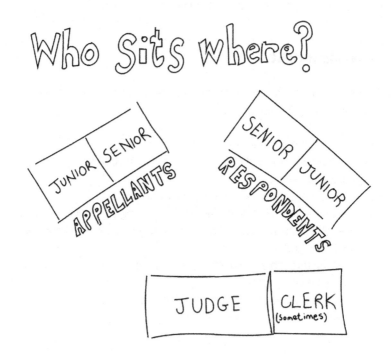

Figure 7.3 Moot seating plan

7.9.17 Judicial interventions

Judicial interventions or in other words, judges 'butting in', is the part of mooting that students find most daunting. Images of a relentless judge picking holes in your carefully prepared speech may bring you out in a cold sweat.

Judges are a mixed bag – remember judges of moots can be academic lawyers, solicitors and barristers in practice and also real judges of course. It's worth remembering that most of them have volunteered their time freely because they want to help young lawyers. Hopefully not too many see it as a golden opportunity to torture bright young things!

The key thing about a moot is that it be seen as a conversation – you kick off and then every so often the judge will want to probe a bit deeper, either to clarify the point you are making or to stretch you a little further.

That's not to say that some judges don't enjoy a little sport! They will sometimes force you to disagree with them, so make sure you have the phrases at your fingertips to be able to confidently (but politely) do this.

Make sure you watch your judge very carefully, this will give you some indication of how well your submissions are going down and allow you to adapt accordingly.

GET USED TO USING THE LANGUAGE REQUIRED OF MOOTS BY RESPONDING TO QUESTIONS IN 'REAL LIFE'.

Try these out:

Parents: You are so irresponsible. Why is your mobile phone bill over £150 this month?

Friend: Why have you tagged me in that picture on that website sprawled over the kerb? That was supposed to be private.

Lecturer: That's two weeks in a row you have clearly not prepared for tutorial. You are going to have to resolve this or your classmates will get fed up of 'carrying you'.

Little sister: Please will you take me to see One Direction at Wembley?

Charity collector (chugger?): Do you have a few minutes for Cancer Research?

CATCHING UP WITH OUR FRIENDS . . .

Sienna and Maisy attend a moot final for postgraduates at their law school, hoping to pick up some tips.

Sienna:	Wow these students sound so impressive! I can't imagine ever being able to sound so fluent and knowledgeable. They don't look nervous at all.
Maisy:	No it's all an act – learning all those phrases to use will

	make life easier. I'm looking forward to our assessed moot, just dreading getting on with the research though.
Sienna:	Did you hear that? The judge wasn't convinced by that line of argument at all . . . I would have frozen if the judge said that to me. I'm going to write down what the mooter said in response: '*Indeed my Lord, that is true in the case of Styles v Malik, though I would submit that the present case can be distinguished on the facts*'.
Maisy:	Yeah it was pretty effective – I think that's one of the hardest things to do: disagree with the judge but keep them onside.

Chapter 8
Employability: learn to earn

8.1 INTRODUCTION

Bring on the competition! When you started university you might have been told, or indeed realised yourself, that you are not necessarily competing against your fellow classmates. That said, when it comes to the job market, you are certainly competing against each other and you'll need to demonstrate why you should be selected for a particular position as opposed to your competitor. If you have studied the same course and you have almost the same results, how on earth is an employer going to decide who to select? The employer must look beyond your results to what other skills and/or experiences you have. In other words, employers have to decide if you have the 'X' factor for them to consider taking you on.

You may have the results, you may even have the degree but you may still struggle to make yourself more employable than the next candidate. Every time you have a dreaded assessment, all you'll be able to think about are the words of your lecturers echoing in your ears telling you how important it is for you to do well so that you can be in the running for the best jobs. As frustrating as it is, you will quickly realise that doing well in your assessments is just not enough anymore. You need to set yourself apart from the crowd so that potential employers take notice of you and ensure you position yourself in the best place that you can in the extremely competitive employment market.

8.2 JUGGLE IT!

So getting good grades is just a part of what you need to do in university life. How are you going to set yourself apart from the crowd and gain these extra skills? You basically need to perform a juggling act and keep a lot of balls in the air. You'll need to focus on your academic development while simultaneously concentrating on your personal and professional development. Since so many students achieve good grades, employers look at what else you can bring to the table and whether this fits in with their work environment. These extras make you more 'employable'. These other things are less prescribed and employers do not really tell you what exactly they are looking for, they know it when they see it. Fear not though – this is a good thing. You then have control over what skills you are going to develop so you can be more original than the next candidate.

8.3 OWN IT!

Wow . . . studying is hard enough! Is this extra stuff just not too much extra pressure? It is very tough to secure that all-elusive training contract, pupillage, graduate scheme or whatever other role you are thinking about, so if you want it you have to take ownership of your employability.

Most universities have a department dedicated to helping students develop their career paths and their employability level. You will find that there is an abundant array of tools and apps out there that will help you manage your personal development which includes monitoring your employability skills. Do not forget however, that your degree may already incorporate personal development planning within your studies directly. A law degree in itself equips you with many skills that employers look for but you need to be adept at translating them into skills that employers value and using a personal development tool can help you do just that.

So you need to develop your employability skills in order for you to be able to secure employment and to prepare you for the big bad world out there. The employment process usually requires you to fill out an application form and attend an interview. Sometimes you may even be required to attend two interviews and/or an assessment day. It is therefore imperative that you have everything in your armoury to position you in the best light at every stage. Your employability skills will be pivotal in achieving this.

There is not one particular characteristic that employers are looking for and that is the key thing to remember. Employers will remember you for being different.

THINKING POINT

Put yourself in the position of an employer who is looking to hire someone new. You and your fellow classmate apply for the position. You and your classmate have both studied the same course and achieved almost the same results. You are both confident and interview really well. How is the employer going to decide who to select? The candidate with something 'extra' will no doubt stand ahead of the candidate without. Your classmate has travelled in their summer holidays, undertaken charity work and started to learn Mandarin. You have undertaken some charity work for a portion of your summer holidays. Who would you hire and why?

8.4 LOST IN TRANSLATION?

Have you ever felt that application forms and employers at interviews speak gobbledygook? What is that you're expected to say? Do they speak in a language that you cannot understand? If so, then you need to learn how to speak the employment lingo, developing skills that speak to potential employers in a language that they understand so that they can recognise the value that you can bring to their company.

Remember, employers pay for skills and talent that employees bring to the company and if they cannot see these in you they are unlikely to consider you for a position. These are skills that you take with you from your education environment to your work environment. These skills are sometimes referred to as *transferable* skills.

Table 8.1 Examples of transferable skills

Transferable skill	Translation
Good time management	Manages responsibilities well, balances conflicting demands on time and prioritises work
Meet deadlines	Punctual, takes work seriously and has the ability to manage workload and time
Problem solving	Unfazed by challenges, logical thinker and resourceful
Organise projects	Has leadership skills, anticipates problems, forward thinking, good time-management skills, good administration skills and can manage/work within a team
Organisation skills	Manages and co-ordinates tasks and others as appropriate, can prioritise and delegate work using own judgment
Work independently	Plans time and workload well, thinks through work objectives, meets targets without supervision, performs delegated tasks and is responsible
Delegate tasks	Prioritises responsibilities, manages time well and recognises strengths in team members
Team player	Appreciates the efficiency of working in a team to achieve common goals, recognises strengths in others, good communication skills, listens well, contributes to achieving targets and is reliable
Effective communicator	Conveys ideas clearly and accurately in a variety of situations both verbally and in writing to own team and external colleagues
Decision making	Makes appropriate decisions when presented with alternatives which suit the situation, thinks logically and can make decisions in a timely fashion
Good researcher	Finds relevant information quickly, asks the right research questions, deciphers and interprets information discerning between reliable and unreliable sources, conveys findings to others
Public speaking	Articulate, confident in speaking to an audience, able to vocalise different lines of argument
Analytical	Processes information to make decisions based on that information, manages a large amount of content to identify important/relevant information within it
Logical reasoning	Thinks clearly through situations to assess the strengths and weaknesses of the information to arrive at a reasoned conclusion, can demonstrate the reasoning behind the conclusion or decision and has confidence to stand by decisions made
Persuasive	Influences others by both the strength and logic of their argument, as well as diplomacy
Plan ahead	Good time-management skills, target based and has long-term vision

While most of you will be able to list an array of such transferrable skills, are you able to convince a potential employer that you actually possess a good grasp of these skills? You must ensure that these abilities do not become lost in translation – you know you have the right skills but do employers recognise that you have them? You must be clear on (a) what employers generally understand and look for in a particular skill; and (b) demonstrate with clear examples the use or display of such a skill. Saying that you possess these skills will never be enough. Employers will look for evidence of such skills on paper, i.e. your CV and application form and in person, i.e. in an interview and/or assessment day. Do not just throw these words around willy-nilly in application forms or at interviews thinking that they will be accepted; employers translate these words in a particular way as set out in Table 8.1 and they want to see *evidence* of these talents. If you understand the meaning of these skills you will be better placed to offer examples of when you have demonstrated or exercised them and therefore convince an employer that you possess these skills.

So what are some examples of transferable skills that employers look for? Table 8.1 shows a non-exhaustive list of some of these and most importantly what they understand by these skills. Always think to yourself: *'what can I bring to the company and offer as an employee?'* Be careful to research the career path and the company that you are applying to so that you can match the skills required for the role with the skills that you possess. If these cannot be paired up significantly, you may want to think again about applying for the role as it may not be suitable for you. If, however, there is a good match between the skills you possess and the skills required for the role, then make sure that the employer can see this and that it does not get lost in translation. Offer clear examples of when you have displayed such skills, not simply stating you possess them.

8.5 SELL IT!

Now that you understand the employer viewpoint on such skills, you must turn your attention to convincing an employer that you have such capabilities. Do not dismiss experience and skills gained from even the smallest job: the chances are that you might not have a great deal of experience so you have to wring out as much as possible from the experiences that you have gained. In other words you need to sell it! You have to sell the fact that you have these abilities and that you are prepared to develop these skills further. So for every skill that you are claiming to have, you need to provide specific evidence of it by giving examples of scenarios where you have used or applied the skill. Beware though and be prepared; do not assume that employers will not check. For instance, if you claim to have written a document for a lawyer when you were on work experience, the employer will cross-check this with your CV and ask you questions about it.

8.6 TAKE IT!

Most law schools will go out of their way to host a number of employer and career events for students to connect with potential employers. These can come in a number of forms. They may be law fairs, recruitment events, talks organised by employers on a particular subject, or they can be talks organised by the careers service on how to complete application forms. These events are not to be missed. You need to take up as many of these opportunities as you can.

These are golden opportunities to learn about particular industries and employers. Such events will help you to better understand and learn what employers are looking for in an employee. Employees at employer events can also give you a little 'insider' information on how to dress up your application form. You may also want to ask the employee representing the company if they would be willing to respond to some questions later on over email. Sometimes you think of something about the company later on, and it would be great to know that there is someone who is able to help you. Does it make sense to miss such opportunities? What is more, you should aim to create a positive lasting impression on the employer, meaning that they may just remember your name when they are sifting through hordes of application forms. This really does demonstrate enthusiasm and commitment to the company, which might be something you can bring up at interview (for example by offering the name of the person that you met at the employer event, and perhaps even explain what you discussed). This type of activity is sometimes referred to as networking, as you are building up a network of contacts.

8.7 APPLY IT!

Ever heard the phrase 'looks good on paper'? Well that is what you have to do when it comes to completing application forms for jobs. Having started to develop your employability skills you now need to sell these skills on paper.

No two application forms will look the same nor should they. You are trying to stand out from the crowd and if you are doing this successfully, your application forms should look different to others. There is not enough scope in this chapter to go through what an application form should look like, but there are some top tips that you should use as a guide when completing an application form (see Table 8.2).

8.7.1 Application form top tips

Table 8.2

Top tip	Translation
1 Check the deadline for when you need to submit the form	Good time management and working independently
2 Read through the form thoroughly and make sure that you understand what each question is asking before you start filling it out	Planning ahead and organisation skills
3 Use spider diagrams or other such tools to plan each answer or section thinking about examples that will support your assertions	Logical thinking
4 Support each of your assertions with specific examples	Logical thinking and persuasive
5 Re-read your complete form and check for any errors	Good communicator

8.8 WATCH IT!

Watch what you write on social media websites! Oh yes we need a whole section on this one. You should assume that if you are putting something on social media or are connected on social media with something questionable, potential employers and/or their clients may find out. Use your judgment. Remember, employers are not divorced from reality; they too will probably have a social media presence and the resources to carry out their due diligence on potential candidates. They will check how potential candidates have portrayed themselves and their public image. Candidates should have a suitable social media image. Remember, employers will check whether the social media image of a candidate could in any way harm the image of the company. You should consider reviewing your social media profile and be sure that you are happy with this image. Ask yourself whether a potential employer would want to be associated with your social media image.

THINKING POINT

Put yourself in the shoes of potential employers who have found the following on social media websites:

(i)   A potential employee is photographed drunk sprawled on the curb in a photo. The potential employee made sure that they were not tagged in the photo yet the employer has managed to find them.

(ii)   A potential employee has noted what they think about the current political party in power.

(iii) A potential employee has posted scathing views about a big corporation – this corporation is a new client of the firm.

(iv)   A potential employee with a profile that has not been updated for three years and has had no activity.

Employers do not want you to be out of touch and delete your social media profiles altogether but they want you to think about maintaining the image of the company and not put anything on there that could bring the company into disrepute. In fact, social media use has many benefits, but used wrongly it can have a damning impact on the company's image.

8.9 GIVE BACK!

Your institution will no doubt host alumni events, which can be particularly eye opening. Wait though, what does alumni even mean? Alumnus refers to a former student of a particular institution. So when we talk about alumni we are talking about a group of former students who have attended a particular institution.

Alumni events are those where students who have graduated from your institution come back to talk to current students about their journey: essentially how they got to their current positions. Two things to note: first, alumni who give up their time in this way do so because they have experience and, some might even say, wisdom that they feel it is important to share with the next generation; and second, they have connections with various employers and can guide and advise you on how to make your applications. These events are invaluable since alumni are offering their advice on what they did or would do differently when they were in your position. You would be mad to miss such opportunities.

8.10 EMPLOY IT!

We then urge you to employ the advice that we have given here in order to make sure that your employability skills are at their best! Yes life at university is hard enough with studying, exams and coursework deadlines, but those who invest in their employability will be those who stand out to employers. It is often said, and will be repeated here, university is not all about study; it is an education both in your subject area and in life!

We finish by helping you to develop an action plan for your employability.

TOP TIPS FOR EMPLOYABILITY

- Do not take your eye off the ball with your studies – achieving the right grades is the first step.
- Become a regular at your careers department.
- Develop your personal development plan and regularly add to it.
- Make a plan for how to develop skills or items on your personal development plan.
- Familiarise yourself with deadlines for application forms.
- Note examples of when you have developed or used a transferable skill that you can later incorporate into an application form.

CATCHING UP WITH OUR FRIENDS . . .

Ashwin has always wanted to become a solicitor. He has known from the moment that he started his degree that he wants to do everything possible to secure a vacation scheme and thereafter a training contract. Ashwin visits his university's careers department who advise him to keep a record of his personal development.

He creates his plan using a template provided by the career's department:

Table 8.3 Example of a personal development plan

Skill?	Written communication	Verbal communication
How can I develop it?	Practise through writing for the Lawbore website; submit voluntary coursework for my modules	Apply to participate in more mooting competitions through my Inns of Court
Are there any difficulties?	Need to receive feedback in order to understand how to improve my written skills	Being accepted to participate but the application process would provide me with a further opportunity to practise my written skills
When?	Next 2 months	Next 2 months

Ashwin then refers to some of the application forms that he will be completing over the course of the next couple of months and draws a spider diagram in black of all of the skills that the firms are looking for. Then, in red, he adds examples of things that he has done, which illustrate his grasp of that skill. He then makes short notes on each of those skills. One of those is his written communication skills:

- Written communication:

    - I have developed excellent communication skills though my experience at Friday's Solicitors where I drafted client letters, which were reviewed by my supervisor. I learnt the importance of writing clearly, concisely and the importance of writing unequivocally and I have since then used this advice in my written work at university and adopted this advice when I am speaking in public.

Chapter 9
Revision and exams: law, eat, sleep, repeat

9.1 INTRODUCTION

Be honest with us, are you reading this chapter because the revision period has already started? We hope this isn't the case for you and that you are approaching it in advance of this. Either way, please use the advice in this chapter to make the most of this crucial period in the academic year.

Whether you're an 'attend everything' kind of student (gold star ☺) or 'miss a tutorial every now and again' kind of student, it will have been reassuring to have had some structure in your life. For the entirety of the year you have known when you have lectures and tutorials, what reading and preparation is required for these and been aware of when the deadlines are for each piece of coursework. You can plan your work around these signposts.

Suddenly all this stops and you find yourself in a time of uncertainty, which can be very daunting. You know when your exams are, but you have a good five or six weeks of nothingness prior to this, which you are supposed to spend recapping on the *entire* year and making it stick in your brain. Sound easy?

Sienna: I'm so relieved this year's over.

Brodie: Me too. Freedom finally! I'm going to start going to the gym again, settle in for weeks of box-set bingeing and have some legendary nights out.

Sienna: What about the revision? Aren't you stressed about that? How are you going to get started? I just don't know what to do and if it's even possible to learn everything in time.

Brodie: Hey don't worry. You're not learning the *whole* course remember, you can pick a few topic areas for each subject and just learn the answers for a few practice essays. Simples. Just plan in a couple of hours' revision a day for the time we have. You need to balance out revision with fun; otherwise you'll just implode.

Do you think there's any truth in what Brodie says? We'll come back to this shortly, first let's think about the purpose of the revision period.

ACTIVITY

Make a note of what you think your revision period should be used for and then compare it to what we think it should be used for. You might be surprised.

Your revision period is *not* a time to start learning topics from scratch, it is to deepen your understanding of topics already learnt; clear up any confusion faced during the year; draw links between different parts of the module; identify (and subsequently fill) any gaps; and to reinforce that knowledge via different means (not just reading your lecture notes through 117 times).

The brain is an amazing organ, and you may be surprised once you begin revising just how much information you have actually retained. However, we often don't recognise this because the panic indicated by Sienna kicks in.

Let's look at the basic pieces of information you need to establish before getting started.

9.2 WHEN ARE YOUR EXAMS?

Your exam period can stretch over a few weeks, so it is really important when planning your revision strategy (yes you will have one of these . . . !) to clarify which exam is happening on which date. You might be lucky and have all of these nicely spaced out, but there is always the possibility, thanks to university timetabling pressures, that you'll have them on consecutive days, perhaps even on the same day. This isn't a disaster, but it can feel like one. Many are thrown by two exams on the same day, wondering what they should focus on the day before.

9.3 WHAT FORMAT WILL THEY TAKE?

Be as prepared as you can be – attend any revision session run by your lecturer and read the module handbook. This will mean there are no nasty surprises when you turn that paper over. Many students get flummoxed on the day and end up answering two questions from the same section (a rubric violation), when they should have answered one from each. Or only tackling part A and not part B, for example. See Table 9.1 below for a checklist of the practical aspects of exams.

Table 9.1 Checklist: practical aspects of exams

You need to establish	
1	How many questions will be staring up at you, and how many of those will you have to complete
2	How long you will have to finish the paper
3	Whether different components will feature in the paper: essay-style questions? Problem questions? Multiple-choice section?
4	Whether you are permitted to take any extra materials in with you – this may be a specific textbook or a statute book

9.4 PLANNING FOR REVISION

A task to complete early on is to put together a revision calendar. This is essential, but be very careful not to fall into the quicksand of procrastination – this is your first test of commitment (see Chapter 2 for advice on study skills). It is astonishing the number of students who suddenly discover an artistic streak they lost somewhere in primary school: revision calendars will feature many different coloured pens, stickers, and sparkles. Such dedication will of course take time, and so the first day of your revision period is lost.

9.4.1 Revision calendar top tips

1   *Be realistic* – no one can study every waking hour. You will have regular commitments that can't be changed – part-time work or sports/music clubs you need to attend practice for. These need to be acknowledged and worked into your calendar. Similarly, as Brodie wisely points out, you need to incorporate some time for you to unwind and forget about law altogether. Far better to plan for some rest periods than not meet your targets and then feel like you've failed.

2   *Split your days* – look to package up the time available. Don't slog all day without a break or the quality of your revision will suffer. You may wish to stick with one module all day, or focus on one module in the morning and a different one in the afternoon. Think about what works best for you. Sometimes you may want to start with something you know reasonably well to build up your confidence to give you the drive to get your revision well and truly under way.

3   *Build in some flexibility* – as you get closer to exam days, things have a habit of going a bit pear-shaped. Plan in a couple of free afternoons that week to cater for the unexpected.

4   *Overestimate how long each module will take* – revision always takes a lot longer than you think.

5   *Make it personal to you* – if you're hopeless in the morning and it takes a 10 a.m. lie in and a few strong coffees to get your brain moving then just adapt your calendar accordingly. But be warned, you are likely to have an exam starting at 9 a.m. so if you are not a morning person, be aware that you may well have to deal with early starts. After all, you will need to start work at 9 a.m. when you start that all-important job that you are hoping to secure!

9.4.2 Revision strategies . . . or what do you actually *do* when revising?

Don't fall into the trap of thinking that effective revision is basically reading your notes from the year, and writing them out again . . . and again . . . and again.

Neither is it learning lots of essays off-by-heart.

The aim of revision is to understand a topic well enough that you can adapt that knowledge to any question. This flexibility can only be realised when you have used a variety of different methods to process that information. We know that everyone favours different learning styles, so some people learn better by visual methods, others learn easier when they hear it. There are of course those who are very text dependent. Think back to your lectures and tutorials – the format of these is often deliberately mixed so that your lecturers can engage everyone, regardless of their learning preference. You might participate in a debate as part of the class, the PowerPoint slides may be very image dependent, rather than lots of text or you may learn from listening to each other's presentations on a topic.

You need to keep your revision as interesting as possible if you stand any hope of making something stick. Mix and match different strategies to ensure you keep boredom at bay and guarantee that knowledge is agile – meaning it can be reused confidently, regardless of what question comes your way on Exam Day.

Here are some ideas:

- *Flash cards* – these are great and can be done in the old-fashioned way with those lined landscape record cards or via one of the many apps out there that allow you to create your own tailored set on your phone or tablet. You could create them for key cases – on one side writing bullet points (brief facts, principles established, judge and date) and name on the other, or perhaps for definitions. Illustrations often work really well here too – you can convey a lot via stickmen! Get your friends or family to test you or make dead time (commuting . . . in the bath . . .) count and test yourself.
- *Practice questions from past papers* – these are essential as they get you into the frame of mind required for the actual exam, and highlight what your strengths and weaknesses are. Your lecturers may allow you to send them a practice paper for brief feedback if you ask in advance. It is not always necessary to write the whole paper – sometimes it is useful just to do the planning for that essay under pressure – brainstorm on a piece of A4 paper and then flick back through your notes to see what you have missed.

This has a double value in that you can add in any omissions and stick up on your walls for recapping during the revision period. It takes quite some discipline to set yourself to writing an essay under timed conditions with no reference materials, but the benefits are significant. It can be quite a shock writing for that length of time, particularly if you normally type your notes and then have to handwrite your exam answers. Beware the claw hand!

- *Creating topic mind maps or tables* – often composing a visual representation of your learning makes it easier for you to recall at a later date (say in your exam?). These are very useful for compiling information around topics on one sheet of paper – key cases, issues, relevant research or commentary and matters of debate. You can also use flow charts for certain processes. Have them in a folder or pin them up in the bathroom. You should include anything relevant from your notes, lectures, textbooks and journal articles (see Figure 9.1 for an example).

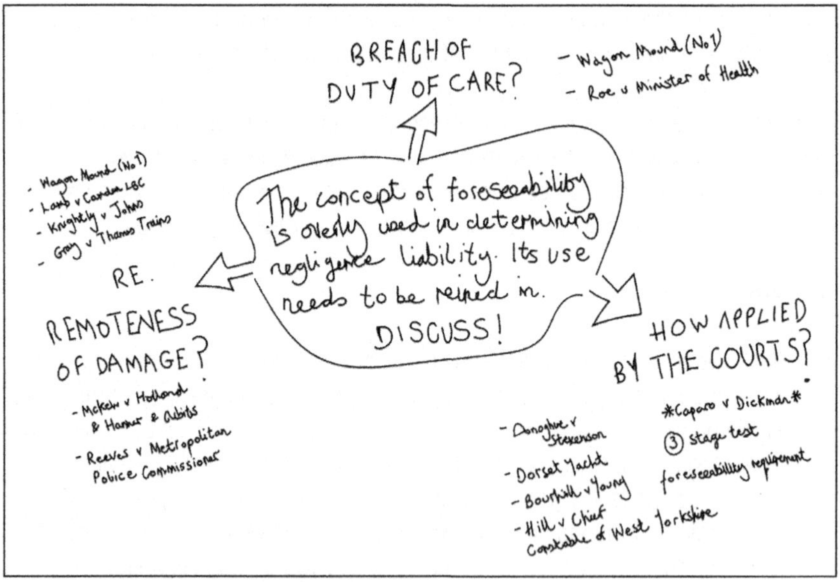

Figure 9.1 Example answer plan

- *Refresh your knowledge* – for topics you covered early in the year, do some quick research for any new developments. You can do this by looking in journals, on the *Guardian* law website or perhaps on Twitter. Double-check your lecture/tutorial handouts for any references to commentary you might have missed. However this cannot take too much time – you have to focus on what you have already learned.

- *Work with others* – don't underestimate how much you can gain from actually vocalising your thoughts. Revision is a lonely activity, and if you have a friend or two who might be willing to team up to exchange knowledge and test each other, then don't hesitate. It might help to have different people to work with for different subjects – this may assist you in the exam, as you'll associate content strongly with individuals, giving you extra triggers for recall. We've also known whole cohorts who have set up Dropbox spaces online to share high scoring essays for revision purposes.
- *Reducing your notes* – although we noted at the beginning of this section that revision isn't about redrafting your existing notes: the process of *reducing* your notes into a condensed super-version is highly worthwhile. This is both in terms of narrowing down to what is most important, and also for creating notes for use during those precious few weeks before the exam.
- *Exploit those velvet tones* – think about voice recording some of your notes and playing them back while you go for a run or drop off to sleep.

9.4.3 What to revise?

Students often feel we're trying to 'catch them out' with exam questions. This couldn't be further from the truth – we write our exam questions in order to give you the best chance to shine. The more students excel, the better we look!

Exam questions are based on the content of the course you have studied: the more of that course you understand, the better equipped you are to pick the questions you will excel at, to answer. Which takes us back to the beginning of this chapter and Brodie's reassuring words to the panicked Sienna. Can you really just revise selected areas and learn the answers to some essays to get through your exams?

We are sure you don't need us to tell you this is a risky strategy. Knowing you have to answer three questions out of a possible six, and only revising four topic areas for a course that has stretched over 20 weeks is leaving a lot to chance. Sometimes, remember, you may have combined topic questions. However, you may feel that revising everything is just not viable, so what do you need to take into account before deciding where to focus your revision within subjects?

9.4.3.1 Your module handbook

This should always be your starting point – it'll help you establish:

(a) the content of your module; and
(b) the relative importance of topics within the module.

Often students forget all about the handbook and dive straight into a revision book they've bought in the hope it contains all the answers. This is a mistake – remember, each university will run a course differently; going into some topics in depth over a few weeks and others omitted entirely. Your lecturers set the questions you'll be answering so it makes sense to base your revision around the handbook they've written, lectures they've given and readings they have suggested. It is likely that 'bigger' topics studied within a module will make an appearance in your exam paper.

9.4.3.2 Your lecture and tutorial notes

You should also consider your coverage of each of the topic areas within a module – was there a week where you couldn't attend the lecture, and never got round to doing the reading for it either? As we've already mentioned, the revision period is not really the time for learning lots of new content, so you need to make a decision whether to knuckle down or discount this one entirely.

9.4.3.3 Peer speculation

Try not to get caught up in the guessing games entered into by some of your peers; no one knows what is going to be in the final paper so it is pointless to waste valuable revision time debating this. Question spotting, where you look at the last few years worth of exam papers and try to work out if there's a pattern you can latch on to, is also ill-advised.

9.4.4 Should I buy revision books?

Revision books have their place but they should not be used in isolation. They are a useful device for flicking through to recap topics, and the Q & A books can help you get a feel for how to answer essay and problem questions if you have only had limited practice on your course. As mentioned above, however, they are generic, so may differ markedly from the content of your university module in terms of detail and focus.

9.5 VIEW FROM THE EXAMINER

This isn't exactly a 'cue violins' moment, but almost as painful as revising, is marking exam scripts. We know in the midst of the hell that is revision, where each morning you wake up groaning at the thought of the day ahead, you can't possibly believe this, but here are a few reflections on the frustrations we face:

(Note: we share this pain in order to get you to think about things from our point of view, not to extract sympathy but to give reasons why you might adapt your work accordingly in the hope of a better mark!)

1   Students who don't answer the question.

> In every revision class you've attended, the warning *'Make sure you read the question!'* is given, and every student thinks *'Yeah yeah . . . of course I'll read the question. Obvious!'* And yet in every exam marked there are many students who just don't do this.
>
> Part of this stems from students learning answers to past essay questions – they see something similar on the exam paper and then regurgitate the one they've memorised, without adaptation. The other part of the phenomenon is where students will focus in on one section of the question, but completely ignore another.
>
> This is very frustrating for us as examiners, as we can only give you credit for what is written down.

2   Students who get carried away with their opinion and forget the law (also students who include *zero primary law*).

> Some subjects are more prone to this than others, but it is not uncommon to see students momentarily forget that they are studying law and write an entire paper aloft their soapbox, sometimes in the complete absence of case law or statute.
>
> While your opinion is encouraged and we look favourably on those who can put forward strong independent arguments, it *must* be supported by authority. Those hours every week spent hearing about cases in

lectures, reading about them in textbooks and discussing them in tutorials – there was a point to this! If you put forward a proposition, then refer to a case to support your view. You don't even need to remember the name – we're happy to accept a super-brief description of the case if the party names escape you.

3   Students who don't plan.

You get into the exam, turn over the paper, and can already hear that clock ticking inside your head. You're desperate to just get writing, so launch straight into your answer.

Not an uncommon scenario for many students, but one that should be avoided at all costs. You must set yourself a strict time for each separate answer before the exam starts, which includes five minutes or so to plan each response. Think of this as a brain dump of facts and ideas, before you turn your attention to the structure.

Students who do not plan end up with muddled, incoherent submissions, usually peppered with asterisks and arrows as they add in extra bits they've forgotten. This is very frustrating for the marker as it is easy to lose track as you attempt to follow these odd tangents sometimes pages later. Any argument loses impact and the marker is left with an unsatisfied feeling of confusion at the end.

Don't put your mark in jeopardy by failing to plan your work – even just a simple spider diagram with key points will give you clarity about how to structure the answer, as well as the main lines of argument and key authorities. It will lend your answer focus and stop you from straying too far from the question set.

4   Students unable to build an argument.

One of the core skills on a law course, and indeed in the legal profession, is that of persuasiveness – being able to convince others that what you are saying is perfectly sensible and that they need to follow your lead. This needs to be explicit in any answer you give in your exam.

This links in with Point 3 above: you can't just leap into an argument, it needs to be planned carefully for maximum effectiveness. You know where you want to end up (in your conclusion), but the points you make to convince the marker along the way have to be calculated. Plan them one by one, deciding upon which authority will best reinforce your point – it could be a case or maybe a piece of commentary you've followed in a journal article.

9.6 STRESS ATTACK

There's no escaping it, most of us dread exams – the thought that the success of your entire year's work is being put to the test over an hour or two is terrifying. Very few people can remain calm in the face of that kind of pressure.

Remember that stress can be a motivator; a little anxiety will push you to work that bit harder. However, when it starts to take over and hinder your focus you may need to seek help, perhaps through the university counselling service. Talk to your family and friends and try to ensure you give yourself time away from revision to take your mind off the upcoming exams temporarily.

9.7 EXAM TOP TIPS

9.7.1 Before the exam

- Be sure to know where you are going and leave plenty of extra time to find the location of where the exam is taking place.
- Take some water and tissues with you.
- Take a good supply of pens with you.
- Take your wristwatch, if you are allowed, so you can keep an eye on the time in the exam for yourself.

9.7.2 Deciding which questions to answer

- Read the rubric (instructions on how many questions to answer) on the front of the exam paper carefully.
- Read all of the questions on the paper several times over before deciding which question you would like to answer.

- Highlight the ones you think you could tackle and start to pull apart the question – circling key words that look like being pivotal to the direction of your answer.
- Scribble quick notes around the question:

    - Questions?
    - Issues?
    - Authorities that spring to mind?

- Decide which you will be answering – re-read the questions, ensuring you're not falling into the trap of imagining it is asking something you've covered in a previous practice question.

9.7.3 The planning process

- Use the first couple of pages in your answer book or the question sheet itself to plan your answers more thoroughly via a brainstorm.
- Ensure you stick to the time you have allocated (in advance) to this part of the process. You may want to limit your planning time to no more than five to eight minutes of your total exam time.
- Resist including everything you know on that general topic area – you are being marked for *relevance* to the question.
- Decide how your ideas would best be structured in order to build the argument – do exactly as you would in a moot, and start with your strongest point.
- Note the actual time and divide the time that you have left equally between each answer that you have to write – in other words, note the time when you need to start answering each question and when you have to stop and move onto answering the next question.

9.7.4 Writing your answer

- Another similarity with mooting – make sure you think through how you signpost throughout, ensuring the marker will feel confident and comfortable with where you are taking him/her in your answer.
- Keep yourself on a tight rein – checking for relevance and ensuring you are *answering the question*.
- If writing by hand, try to keep it legible – we can't mark what we can't read. Different universities will have different policies on what happens in the

event of unintelligible scrawl, you may even have to pay for it to be typed out. It's not always messy handwriting that is a problem, but sometimes size of print.

- Leave a few clear lines after each paragraph so that you can go back and add in information that might come to you later.
- Give yourself time to conclude your answer – don't just leave us hanging.
- Start each answer on a new page – this is good for your confidence and also leaves you some space in the booklet for adding to your answer if something comes to you later on.
- Try to ensure you leave ten minutes or so for re-reading and checking for errors or inconsistencies.

9.7.5 After the exam

- Decide if you want to compare notes of your answers with your fellow students after the exam. Could this boost your confidence or knock you down? Remember you might have more exams coming up so you need to stay focused on those.
- Take some of the rest of the day off or at least a few hours, before you start revising for the next exam.

CATCHING UP WITH OUR FRIENDS . . .

Ashwin is determined to be organised in this academic year, and thinks he'll start getting ready for the revision period by compiling information about cases he has studied on flash cards. He kicks off by looking at a few of the cases that he'll be using within the assessed moot around rectification. Here's what his cards look like!

East v Pantiles (Plant Hire) Ltd (1981) 263 EG 61

- There must be a clear mistake.
- What should the correction be?
- Qualified by *Chartbrook*.

Chartbrook Ltd v Permission Homes Ltd [2009] 1 AC 1101

- Correction by construction is part of the law on rectification not something separate – it falls within the overall interpretation exercise.

- The court can be persuaded to look beyond the agreement itself and take into account the background and context to the agreement when interpreting the agreement.

Agip SpA v Navigazione Alta Italia SpA (The Nai Genova and the Nai Superba) [1984] 1 Lloyd's Rep 353

- The court will consider whether the defendant had actual knowledge of the existence of the relevant mistake at the point of contract.
- Rectification is an appropriate remedy if the defendant had actual knowledge of the mistake at the relevant time.
- Does it appear that the contract does not accurately represent the true agreement of the parties? Would the contract, if rectified, accurately reflect the true agreement of the parties at the point of contract?

Index